The Young Christian at University

Overcoming Challenges as a Student

HAYFORD AKOWUAH

authorHOUSE®

AuthorHouse™ UK
1663 Liberty Drive
Bloomington, IN 47403 USA
www.authorhouse.co.uk
Phone: 0800.197.4150

© *2017 Hayford Akowuah. All rights reserved.*

No part of this book may be reproduced, stored in a retrieval system, or transmitted by any means without the written permission of the author.

THE HOLY BIBLE, NEW INTERNATIONAL VERSION®, NIV® Copyright © 1973, 1978, 1984, 2011 by Biblica, Inc.® Used by permission. All rights reserved worldwide.

Scripture taken from the New King James Version®. Copyright © 1982 by Thomas Nelson. Used by permission. All rights reserved.

Scripture quotations marked (NLT) are taken from the Holy Bible, New Living Translation, copyright © 1996, 2004, 2007 by Tyndale House Foundation. Used by permission of Tyndale House Publishers, Inc., Carol Stream, Illinois 60188. All rights reserved.

The ESV® Bible (The Holy Bible, English Standard Version®). ESV® Permanent Text Edition® (2016). Copyright © 2001 by Crossway, a publishing ministry of Good News Publishers. The ESV® text has been reproduced in cooperation with and by permission of Good News Publishers. Unauthorized reproduction of this publication is prohibited. All rights reserved.

Copyright © 2015 by The Lockman Foundation, La Habra, CA 90631. All rights reserved.

Holman Christian Standard Bible®
Copyright © 1999, 2000, 2002, 2003, 2009 by Holman Bible Publishers. Used with permission by Holman Bible Publishers, Nashville, Tennessee. All rights reserved.

Published by AuthorHouse 09/15/2017

ISBN: 978-1-5462-8200-6 (sc)
ISBN: 978-1-5462-8201-3 (e)

Print information available on the last page.

Any people depicted in stock imagery provided by Thinkstock are models, and such images are being used for illustrative purposes only. Certain stock imagery © Thinkstock.

This book is printed on acid-free paper.

Because of the dynamic nature of the Internet, any web addresses or links contained in this book may have changed since publication and may no longer be valid. The views expressed in this work are solely those of the author and do not necessarily reflect the views of the publisher, and the publisher hereby disclaims any responsibility for them.

Dedications

I would like to dedicate this book, first to the LORD God Almighty for His guidance and wisdom that made this book a reality. He's the one that gave me the vision and plan for this book so all I can do is give it back to Him - He deserves all the glory!

Secondly, I would also like to dedicate the book to my friend (Lillian Esianor) who has played a very important and instrumental part of making this book come to be. When God gives you a vision, He sends destiny helpers to make the vision come to pass. Had it not been for Lillian constantly encouraging me to get started and checking in to make sure I finished the book, it would still be a vision, not a reality; just like many other world-changing, God-given ideas that we often push on the back burner. It is my prayer that you live to fulfil every plan that God has for you and may He cause you to be outstanding among ten thousand.

Acknowledgements

All the glory, honour and adoration to the Most High God for the great things He has done! I cannot take credit for this book because I am merely a vessel and the LORD has manifested Himself through me. "It is because of Him that you are in Christ Jesus, who has become for us wisdom from God - that is, our righteousness, holiness and redemption. Therefore, as it is written: "Let the one who boasts boast in the LORD"" – 1 Corinthians 1:30-31 [NIV].

I would like to thank my family for the love and support they've shown me during this project. It hasn't been easy but they've constantly been there for me and encouraged me when I felt like giving up.

I would also like to take this opportunity to thank all the amazing friends that God gave me. The love and support I have received for this book has been overwhelming. The constant checking up on the progress of this project has been surprising. God bless you all and I pray that your labour will never be in vain.

A special thank you to Sharon Tembo (singer/songwriter, worship leader and chart-topping gospel recording artist). She was the main editor for this book and the LORD has used her immensely to develop this project. Thank you so much for availing yourself even with your busy schedule. May God continue you to bless and prosper you in all your endeavours.

A huge thank you to COP-UK; particularly to the Leicester and Birmingham districts for their prayers, guidance and teachings that have made me the man that I am today. I appreciate every single pastor, elder and member that has made a great impact in my life during my time at University.

I take a great pleasure in saying thank you to 'Author House UK'. When I began writing this book, I knew nothing about publishing but God blessed me with a wonderful team who have helped and walked me through the entire process - from the very beginning, right up to the release of this book. Thank you to my publishing consultant (Jud Cure), the check-in coordinator (Eric Porton) and the entire team at Author House UK. God bless you all.

Finally, to all my readers - I pray that this book encourages you to live boldly and unashamedly in your true identity as a child of God during your time at university and for the rest of your life. I pray that it also inspires you to pursue your God-given dreams and work hard as a diligent steward of the course God has placed you in; remember that all things are possible through Christ, who is your strength - so never give up. Don't neglect your relationship with God; but rather, hold fast to Him and His Word, submit under His power & authority - then you will truly be unstoppable as you pursue His purpose for your life. - "But those who wait on the LORD shall renew their strength; they shall mount up with wings like eagles, they shall run and not be weary, they shall walk and not faint" – Isaiah 40:31 [NKJV].

Contents

Dedications v
Acknowledgements vii
Introduction xi

Chapter 1   God Comes First! 1
Chapter 2   Finding Your Identity 4
Chapter 3   Friendships and Acquaintances 9
Chapter 4   Overcoming Addictions 12
Chapter 5   Let Go of The Past 15
Chapter 6   Go Back to Your First Love 18
Chapter 7   Be an Example of Christ in Your University 22
Chapter 8   You Are There For A Purpose 25
Chapter 9   You Are a Leader 29
Chapter 10 Prayer as a Weapon 32
Chapter 11 Live by Faith, Not by Sight 37
Chapter 12 It's Only by His Grace 39
Chapter 13 Study to Show Yourself Approved 42

Introduction

For those who decide to take the route to their future via university, it is the most exciting, yet challenging stage in life as the transition from adolescence to adulthood occurs. In addition to being a young person, being a Christian (like myself) at university is not always a walk in the park. University is the place where - if you're not careful - you may come to the brink of an identity crisis as your morals & beliefs are questioned and your faith tested. Many people fail this test of faith because of the pressures associated with fitting in with peers or societal expectations which are classed as the "norm". However, as a child of God, know that you are not meant to fit society's glove of normalcy; as the Word of God instructs us in Romans 12:2 - "do not conform to the pattern of this world, but be transformed by the renewing of your mind. Then you will be able to test and approve what God's will is – His good, pleasing and perfect will" (NIV).

Don't get me wrong though; aside from the struggles that come with being a Christian at university, there are also good times, lots of excitement and life-long memories to be made! God wants you to enjoy this life; and when you learn how to enjoy it WITH Him, as opposed to seeking worldly "enjoyment", you'll come to find that nothing can compare with the joy and wholeness He brings! University is a great terrain in which you can learn just how amazing God is and how amazing He thinks you are as you discover your identity in Him! This period of your life is a period of growth. You will face many different types of situations, come across all types of people and be put in positions where you will have to make decisions that will either make you or break you; but there's nothing to fear or be anxious about because you are being prepared for the real world and the coming seasons of your life. Each day at university presents new opportunities for growth; so, make sure you grab as many of them as possible! University is the place where we see boys become men and girls become women; however, we weren't created to just be ordinary men or women but world-changing, light-shining, righteous men and women of God. Irrespective of the hurdles and challenges you may face at university, if you take it in your stride and remain in the LORD, then you will overcome the trials and temptations that come your way! "I have told you these things, so that in me you may have peace. In this world, you will have trouble. But take heart! I have overcome the world" - John 16:33 (NIV). This is God's assurance that, though your faith may come into question during your time of studies - He who has called YOU is faithful to redeem you when you call upon Him.

In this book, I am going share some of my university experiences alongside the conceptual perceptions of university "norms" and how a young Christian can grow, overcome temptations and complete university, having come out victorious in Christ!

Chapter One

GOD COMES FIRST!

For most of us, university is the first time we leave home. A lot of us have not experienced an independent lifestyle prior to university and so, we get caught up in the excitement of freedom and forget the morals and Christian values that our parents worked so hard to instil in us over the years once we get there. It becomes so easy to neglect God and start behaving like children of the world; going to all kinds of parties and associating ourselves with things that we know don't please God.

University is a place where we all encounter many situations that may lead us to conform to the patterns of the world, disguised as the 'university lifestyle'. Some people start smoking, drinking or even sleeping around; these are just a few examples of what are classed as the "norm" in the life of a university student. However, as children of God we must remember this is NOT our normality… Personally, my issue was with girls. I found myself doing things with girls that I wouldn't normally do back home; not because I was pursuing them, but because I got comfortable – comfortable thinking that my life was okay the way it was and forgetting about The God that brought me to university in the first place. In my comfort is where I encountered many temptations; many of us think we are strong until we are faced with temptations – I can honestly say that this was a real test of my self-control and showed me the level of strength I was *really* operating at.

God wants us to acknowledge that without Him we are weak, but also understand that in our weakness, He is our strength. The battles we face at university are not of the world, they are spiritual and these spiritual battles are going on because the devil wants to distract you from what God has planned for your life in university. Thankfully, God lets us know in 2 Corinthians 10:4 that, "the weapons we fight with are not of the world. On the contrary, they have divine power to demolish strongholds" [NIV]. We cannot fight spiritual battles with our physical bodies; they must be fought in the spirit with a superior power, which is the Spirit of God. One major tactic that the devil tries to enforce is that of distraction. It's so easy to get caught up in the busyness of life - you may have those periods where you spend time with God daily, but as the demand for your time increases - with assignments/deadlines, maintaining a social life, sleep, family and employment etc. - you can very easily miss one day of quiet time with the LORD. That one day can then turn into a week without quiet time, then a month - eventually you find yourself backslidden and far from God. This is why God wants us to put Him first in everything. Time spent with Him makes you aware of the enemy's devices, helps you discern the attacks of the enemy in your life and positions you to fight in the spirit. Just know that when everything tries to compete with God for your time, you need to stop and get your priorities in order - everything else needs to come *after* God. Plan your day around God - don't just fit God in a 'convenient' time slot in your day. Always fix your eyes on Jesus so that the devil can't grab your attention with perishable things. Make sure you stay focused and connected to Him to overcome the enemy. The scripture says in Matthew 6:33, "…seek first the Kingdom of God and His righteousness, and all these things shall be given to you" [KJV]. If you put God first in everything… He will ensure that you succeed in everything you do. The majority of the time, we even allow our problems to distract us from who God is - we try and sort them out by ourselves in our own understanding or by even going to others for help rather than straight to God! How often do you share your problems with your friends before even speaking to God about them? Moreover, instead of telling your friends about how big your problems are you should be telling your problems how big your God is!

How can you be defeated if you face your Heavenly Father in prayer daily before leaving the house? As Christians, our aim should be to have an intimate relationship with God – in fact, many of us claim to desire this. However, actions speak louder than words; can you truthfully say that you put in the effort necessary to achieve such a relationship with Him? At times, we even struggle to communicate with God on a daily basis, yet He still so deeply desires to spend time with us… He's always there, doing His part – but, remember that relationships are a two-way affair. God is a jealous God and doesn't want us to put anything before Him. Sometimes, the very thing we pray for, becomes a god to us once we receive it, then we start making excuses and spending less time with God; until eventually, we forget who we are, end up straying further away from Him and deeper into the world. If we want to be successful at university and fulfil the will of God for our lives in university, we must put God first in everything!

Chapter Two

FINDING YOUR IDENTITY

If you're not careful, university is a place where you can easily get lost and follow the crowd if you haven't found yourself as a person and aren't secure in who you are. Identity is very important for each person because it is what defines you as an individual. Identity is about understanding who God says you are and who He has called you to be, as well as understanding your personal values, strengths and weaknesses.

When it comes to the subject of identity, the names we possess are probably the very first thing that come to mind. Did you know that a person's name alone can have significant impact on their behaviour? For example, you may find that individuals with names that signify greatness may just naturally walk in greatness, whereas other names with negative connotations or painful meanings behind them, may negatively affect an individual. For this reason, it is important for every individual to find out the meaning or the characteristics associated with their names; However, if you happen to discover negative connotations associated with your name, there's nothing to worry about. You must know that names are very important to God; He knows that there is power in names and He is very much so in the business of changing them! There are many instances in the Bible where God changed the names of people when He was revealing their true identity to them. For example, in Genesis 17:5 and 15 we find Abram's name [meaning 'Father is High'] being changed to Abraham [meaning 'father of a multitude'] and Sarai's name [meaning 'my princess'] to Sarah [meaning 'mother of nations']. God changing their names had to do with the covenant and purpose placed on their lives.

Start observing the patterns in your life. If you find that negative cycles of certain behaviours, failures or even lifestyle factors (such as poverty) keep recurring, it's an indication that something needs to be broken in the spiritual. There is power in the tongue [Proverbs 18:21] so pay close attention to the names you call yourself. If you're constantly calling yourself *'stupid'* or *'broke'*, for example, don't be surprised if you find yourself always failing your exams or having no money… A lot of times we curse ourselves without realising the impact our words are having. Remember - there is power in the words we speak!

Another factor to consider is your birth name. Your parents may give you one name, but if it's not in line with who God says you are and His purpose for you, you don't have to walk through life with the weight of those undesirable connotations upon your life. God created you and knows you better than anybody else does. He even knows you better than you know yourself. So, He is willing and ready to redeem you to your true identity – you just have to seek Him to receive all that He has for you. One person in the bible that chose not to suffer at the expense of his birth name was a man named Jabez [meaning 'sorrow']. 1 Chronicles 4:9 tells us that his mother called him this "because his birth had been so painful" [NLT]. Jabez refused a life governed by pain and sorrow just because of his name, as a result, he lifted this prayer to God: "Oh, that you would bless me and expand my territory! Please be with me in all that I do, and keep me from all trouble and pain!" – 1 Chronicles 4:10 [NLT]. This same verse also tells us that "God granted his request". So, there you have it, if you seek Him and bring your requests before Him, He is ready and able to grant you a turnaround in your life. Like Jabez, will you choose not to succumb to a cursed life? There is no name that God cannot change or reverse the negative effects of. That also goes for the negative names people call you in relation to the past sins and mistakes that you made. People may refer to you as *"the girl who did this"* or *"the guy who did that"* – they may think you are not capable of changing; but remember, when you come to Christ and become born again, you are a new creation. Because of His redeeming love, an encounter with God cultivates change and transformation; as a result, the more you grow in Him, the more you become like Christ and stop doing the things you used to do – so really, any reference to you based on your former nature carries no weight because what God says about you carries more weight than any other claim, accusation or opinion. Isaiah 43:1 tells us briefly about Jacob's name change; ""But now, thus says the LORD, who created you, O Jacob, And He who formed you, O Israel: "Fear not, for I have redeemed you; I have called you by your name; You are Mine"" [NKJV]. Jacob's name translates to 'supplanter', this describes someone who "overtakes, trips up or takes the place of someone else by force or deceitfulness" – if you make yourself familiar with his story in Genesis, you'll find that he had a history of deceiving and cheating his older brother Esau. Racking up this kind of reputation could have claimed him the title of a 'trickster' for his entire life. However, he had an encounter with God [Genesis 32:28] and this changed him forever. God redeemed him and gave him the name Israel, meaning 'a prince with God' – this is a perfect demonstration of how God redeems us; your old sinful nature passes away and God reveals to you, how He sees you and who you are in Him – you take on the new Godly nature when you come to Christ [2 Corinthians 5:17]. So, take heart, no matter where you've been and no matter what you've done, your past does not define you. Your Creator wants you to encounter Him so that you can receive His forgiveness, then He can also redeem you and form you into your true self. No sin or past is too dirty for Him to wash away; you are not your mistakes. You are forgiven.

A friend of mine once asked me, *"Who is Hayford? What is unique about him? And what makes him stand out amongst thousands?"* – I began to ponder over these questions and articulate words to describe who I thought I was, but was unable to come up with a clear answer. I realised that I had to go on an identity search and discover who I am. I began to search for the meaning of my name 'Hayford', as well my family background. I also tried looking at my lifestyle, character traits, dreams and aspirations to come to a conclusion that defines who I am – but all that was inconclusive. As much as we'd like to say we know ourselves, we don't actually know ourselves as much as we think we do. We can try studying ourselves – observing our capabilities, personal strengths and weaknesses but this won't give us the full picture of who we truly are. What better way to find out who you are than by asking the One Who created you? Think of it this way, an invention does not determine its own name and purpose – it's the inventor that determines those things.

The inventor also provides an instruction manual with his creation. You are the creation, God is The Creator and His Word (The Holy Bible) is your instruction manual. As you spend time with The Creator and the instruction manual, He begins to reveal your identity and show you who you are – and in turn, your purpose.

Once you know who God says you are, you can confidently walk through life with your identity firmly rooted in Christ. Then, what other people say about you should align with who God has already said you are. If they speak negatively about you, it should provoke you to check yourself to see if you're truly walking in your God-given identity or lead you to go on an identity search if you don't know what God has said. However, if you are purposing in your heart to intentionally walk as who God has called you to be, then negative talk shouldn't sway or dishearten you – it's just a distraction you must pay no mind to, many people accused Jesus of different things because they didn't know who He was but He kept on walking in purpose, as should you.

Additionally, what you say about yourself also has to be in line with what God's Word is saying about you. Sometimes we beat ourselves up about our weaknesses and yet recognizing them is the first step towards making a change. Furthermore, some of your perceived weaknesses can also be strengths in disguise, as I have come to understand. After asking some of my closest friends to describe me using 5 words, they came out with terms like; *accountable, selfless, trustworthy, kind and supportive*. My eyes were opened to how certain traits I perceived to be weaknesses actually doubled up as strengths; for instance, some friends described me as someone who is talkative; but this isn't necessarily bad as they also mentioned how I have impacted their lives through the things I've spoken to them. I also came to realise the kind of influence and impact I was making on people. Jesus did the same thing with His disciples in Matthew 16:15-16 [NLT] and asked: ""… who do you say I am?" Simon Peter answered, "You are the Messiah, the Son of the living God."" – Because Jesus walked confidently and obediently in Who God called Him to be, Simon Peter had no issue in recognizing that Jesus was the Messiah; and in the same way, people should know you by your fruits – your identity should clearly exude from you, with your actions speaking louder than your words or at the very least – because not every single person will understand you – those closest to you should be able to correctly say who you are. If they can't say who you are then perhaps you need to be more intentional about walking with God and in your God-given identity. If you can't boldly say who you are, then perhaps it's time you go on an identity search, by seeking God so that you can be confident and certain of who you are.

Chapter Three

FRIENDSHIPS AND ACQUAINTANCES

An acquaintance is someone that you spend time with on occasion; someone you're getting to know, but you don't know them that well yet; they have the potential to become a friend. However, when you really need them, they might not come through.

Friendship is a mutual relationship where both parties can rely on, trust and support one another. A friend is more intimate than an acquaintance; friends know more about each other and tend to share similar interests in one way or another – "Can two walk together, unless they are agreed?" – Amos 3:3 [NKJV]; in general, friends walk together because they have a mutual level of understanding on certain topics; however, where there are constant disagreements in friendship, the relationship can be easily broken.

Your friends are the most influential people in your university life. Whether you would agree with me or not, the truth of the matter of the fact is that you either influence your friends or they influence you in some way. The question is, how are they influencing you? Or how are you influencing them?

When it comes to student life, 1 Corinthians 15:33 holds a truth that you cannot afford to overlook, especially as a young Christian at university; "Do not be misled: "Bad Company corrupts good character"" [NIV]; and indeed, it is true, my time at university allowed me to see such unravel before my own eyes. During university, I met a lot people who were engaging in activities, that as Christians, we ought not to get caught up in ourselves; from smoking weed and taking drugs to sexual immorality and participating in fraudulent behaviour – all because of the company they kept at university. As stated earlier, bad company corrupts good character; hence why it's so important for us to evaluate the company around us and differentiate between our friends and acquaintances because while some people may be in our lives for a lifetime, others are only supposed to be in our lives for a season. Moreover, we must be very careful as to how we choose our friends.

Regardless of whether you're at university or not, it's important that you frequently ask yourself – "*how are my friends impacting me?*" Or "*how am I impacting them?*" Are they the kind of friends that always want to have fun, but when it comes to being serious, they've suddenly got to go? Or are they the type of friends that always want to take but are never willing to give? – In view of all these things, don't forget that whatever standards of measurement you use to evaluate your friends are the same standards you must also use to assess what kind of friend you are yourself – So, take some time to sit back and re-evaluate yourself and your friendship groups, even if that means coming off social media platforms and setting some time aside to focus on other important things and just spend time alone with God; besides, He is the only One who can reveal to you, the kind of friend you're supposed to be, the people that are meant to be in your life and shed light on who you may need to let go of.

Understand that not everyone that is with you is for you, some of your so-called '*friends*' are actually waiting for an opportunity to eliminate you. Therefore, you need the spirit of discernment to be able to recognise who is for you and who is against you. I credit God for the person that I have become today, but I'm also very grateful for the kind of brothers and sisters I met at university. Friends that will not allow you to fall off and backslide; friends that always encourage you and bring out the best in you; friends who delight in your growth, not your downfall. In fact, one of the reasons I have been able to complete this book, was because a friend kept pushing me and constantly kept checking on the progress I was making throughout the writing process. I thank God for such friends! Still, there's a need for every individual to assess their friendship groups; because, like I mentioned earlier, some friends are in your life for a season… and some people's seasons are up – it's time to let them go as they may bring you down rather than build you up.

One reputable example of good friendship in the Bible is that of David and Jonathan in 1 Samuel. There was so much love shared between them that Jonathan would go behind his father's back to inform David of Saul's plan against him to protect him. You would be surprised to find out how many of your peers at university can sit amongst the very people that speak negatively of you, but would not even utter a word in your defence; so, *who* are your *friends*? And are *you* a true friend? "Then Jonathan made a covenant with David because he loved him as his own soul" – 1 Samuel 18:3 [ESV]; Do your friends love you? Do you love your friends? How much are you willing to serve one another? Distinguish and draw the line between your friends and your acquaintances.

Chapter Four

OVERCOMING ADDICTIONS

I know that addiction can be a touchy subject but it is a very important issue that needs to be addressed. Addiction is a stumbling block which if not taken care of as soon as possible, can lead you to stray further away from God - the thing that you're addicted to then becomes your god. Not to mention the very serious implications that will arise in your life because of the addiction and distance from God. Sometimes, we can even find it hard to be honest with ourselves when it comes to admitting that we have an addiction, but I truly believe that the first step to squashing addiction is confessing that you have a problem.

I was introduced to gambling in my final year of college – so, just before I went to university. At first, it didn't seem like an issue – it just seemed like good, casual fun and a quick, easy way to make money. But gradually my mind was getting so consumed with it that I eventually became heavily addicted to gambling. It got to the point that every bit of money that came into my possession had me running to gamble – I always felt the need to try my luck and see if I could double it. Now, those of you who are already at university would agree with me that Student Finance isn't for high maintenance purposes; and once the rent has been paid, there is barely enough to even live on. I guess the fact that I was always buying clothes and shoes didn't help either. Yes, I like dressing up and looking good – but looking good comes at a cost. I would say that the shopping and constant pressure to look "fleeky" – as the youth would say these days – were some of the biggest contributing factors to my gambling problem at university. Moreover, I had no job at the time due to studying a very demanding course. During this season, I would go to the betting shop from time to time; some days I was very lucky and other days, not so much. In those instances, I would leave the shop feeling depressed and would only think negative thoughts. This carried on for a while and I knew it was getting out of hand. I tried to stop a few times but failed every time because I was trying to do it in my own strength without God and without moral support. Because I was so embarrassed about my problem I couldn't even share it with my closest friends or seek help.

At church, whenever they gave deliverance alter calls for people with any type of issue, I was always one of the first people to get up. After receiving prayer, I would stay away from gambling for weeks; sometimes months... but because I wasn't engaging with God for healing in those weeks/months, it became easy for me to turn back to my addiction whenever I needed something badly – then I was back to square one. I even made excuses for myself about my gambling issue by convincing myself that it was "*the answer to my problems*" and that it was my "*only way of surviving*" at university; but really, it just got me in further problems and I was depending so much on myself that I had forgotten about the God who brought me to university in the first place.

I finally got to a point where I was willing to do anything to stop gambling because I realized that it had a hold over me and was controlling my life. Although I acknowledged the spiritual aspect to my issue, I also had to acknowledge the physical side and make a conscious decision not to go back to it. Despite this revelation, I kept on gambling because I was still "*winning*"; until one day, when I lost a huge sum of money. As soon as I left the shop, I made a promise to myself and to God; I said it out loud, that I would never enter a betting shop, ever again and I never looked back since. At this point, I became very angry with myself but most importantly, I became aware of what I had been getting myself into and realized that I had been struggling, fighting this battle on my own. I became tired of the situation and so, resolved to invite God into it. "Ask and it will be given to you; seek and you will find; knock and the door will be opened to you" – Matthew 7:7 [NIV]. God is ever ready and His arms are always opened to receive you. All you have to do is seek Him and you will find Him. I sought the LORD and I found Him; He came to my aid and rescued me.

You're probably thinking about your own addictions; the things that you have been struggling to give up, the things that you've been drowning in – the very things that you know have been corrupting you inwardly. Yes, you can pray about it... but sometimes the solution is very simple, God already delivered and set you free a long time ago; when Jesus died on the cross. You have already been healed mentally, physically spiritually and emotionally; all you have to do is take a step of faith and make a conscious decision – for yourself – to flee from the devil and not to go back to those poisonous habits that have been destroying you for so long. As a born-again Christian, the Spirit of God living inside of you empowers you to overcome sin, but until you purpose it in your heart and make that conscious decision, you will always be subjected to a vicious cycle of bondage and addiction to that "thing" - whatever it may be, whether gossip, gambling, toxic relationships, pornography, drugs, sex/fornication or fraud etc. Don't make excuses for yourself that make you feel better about living comfortable in your sin, like I did when I thought gambling was my only means of provision; when it comes to many of these other addictions, examples of certain excuses commonly thrown around are – *"I can't help it"*, *"I'm on a journey, I'm going through a process"*, *"God knows my heart"*, *"I will ease myself away from it and stop gradually"* and *"everyone else is doing it"*, etc. As far as your freedom is concerned, God has already done His part and deposited His Spirit within you; it is now up to you to take the necessary steps towards freedom, without holding back and carry on with boldness in your true identity in Christ.

Chapter Five

LET GO OF THE PAST

Everyone has some memories from the past that they may not necessarily be proud of; however, your past does not define who you are now – neither does it define your future. We can rest assured that, regardless of the mistakes we've made, we can always grow and learn from them. Just as a child will have to go through certain things to know what is not good for them, so it is with us. As children explore, they tend to put their hands in anything and on everything, simply because they do not know or understand the object that has intrigued them. An example is with candles; a child may be attracted to the bright light of a candle flame – however, because they have no idea whatsoever of the impending danger associated with touching this glowing thing that fascinates them so much, they proceed to touch the flame and of course we all know that tears and screaming follow. Once that child gets injured and experiences that burn, they learn their lesson and acknowledge that fire is not something to be played with. Such is the concept of life – if we knew or understood the consequences of some of the things we engage ourselves in or even entertain in our lives, would we still do them? Nevertheless, everything we go through teaches us a lesson and prepares us for similar obstacles that we may face in the future. One of the signs of growth is being able to turn from the past and focus on the future that God has promised you. The first step of letting go is to forgive yourself, because God has already forgiven you and no longer sees you as a sinner – "Therefore, if anyone is in Christ, he is a new creation; old things have passed away; behold, all things have become new" – 2 Corinthians 5:17 [NKJV].

What we need to understand is that, blood symbolises life [Genesis 9:4] and that sin results in death; for the scripture tells us in Romans 6:23 that "...the wages of sin is death" [NIV]. What this means is that, where sin is, blood must be shed for the forgiveness of sin. For this reason, in the past, animals were killed as sacrifices and their blood was shed and offered up for the atonement of sin. Atonement, in biblical terms, refers to the forgiveness of sins by shed blood. Jesus came to earth as the ultimate sacrifice for the payment of our sins, to replace the animal sacrifices once and for all. The animal blood would only cleanse on a surface level; so, people still continued living in sin. On the other hand, the blood of Jesus - which is more powerful - cleanses us inwardly as well, and breaks the curse of sin and darkness for good. Therefore, we are able to let go of our sinful past. "For He made Him who knew no sin *to be* sin for us, that we may become the righteousness of God in Him" - 2 Corinthians 5:21 [NKJV]. Now that you are a child of God - a new creation - you are the righteousness of God, not by your own efforts but because of the blood of Jesus which was shed for you; so, walk in freedom.

There was a time at university I invited a friend of mine to the campus fellowship that I had been attending and she gave me a very interesting response. She said and I quote, *"I don't want God to think that I'm using Him"*. I smiled and asked her, *"How could you possibly use God?"* She replied, *"I don't want God to think that I only come to Him when I need Him"*. I explained to her that, God wants us to come to Him in our weakness because that is when His Power is made perfect [2 Corinthians 12:9]; it's only when we acknowledge that we are weak and need Him that we come to realise that He is our strength. Hence why Jesus said, "Come unto me, all ye that labour and are heavy laden, and I will give you rest" – Matthew 11:28 [KJV]. Plus, once you encounter His Love and *choose* to surrender to Him wholeheartedly, a relationship begins to develop – you need to understand that God's Love for you is unconditional, there's nothing you can do to earn His Love. You may feel like you're "using Him" but when you shift your mindset from a place of religion – trying to "be good" in your own strength – to a place of relationship – accepting God's Love and understanding the magnitude of Christ's sacrifice – then you'll stop feeling like an outsider and come to a place of true intimacy with God. So, friends, I'd also like to encourage you to give everything to God. As Christ said, "rest" is found in Him – trying to be a "good person" or trying to let go of the past you're not proud of in your own strength is going to get tiring and burn you out; you need Him to move on from anything and everything that has held you back, kept you stuck and kept you stagnant in one place. Just know that everything that is a burden in your life was already carried on the cross when Jesus was nailed to it and died for you. Therefore, you CAN walk in victory knowing that He paid the price.

Sinach – the gospel artist – sang, *"I'm walking in power, I'm walking in miracles, I live a life of favour, because I know who I am"* – Do you know who you are? – You are victorious, you are powerful, you are glorious and you are the son/daughter of the Most High God. So, don't let anyone or anything tell you or make you think otherwise because "He who is in you is greater than he who is in the world" – 1 John 4:4 [NKJV].

Chapter Six

GO BACK TO YOUR FIRST LOVE

The Christian journey is a journey of a lifetime and one which you may fall or slip up from time to time. Especially being in an environment like university where young adults experience an array of constant pressures such as: pressure from society, pressure to succeed and pressure to look a certain way or engage in certain activities. We, as young people, are constantly compared to the standards of success of others which sometimes leads to neglecting our Christian morals and values to pursue success in an ungodly manner. Not only is it the pursuit of earthly success that can cause us to fall, but a range of other factors such as giving into peer pressure, lust of the flesh, lust of the eyes and the pride of life. However, falling isn't the issue – the important thing is to rise back up after the fall; "though a righteous man falls seven times, he will get up, but the wicked will stumble into ruin" – Proverbs 24:16 [HCSB].

Falling does not mean it's the end of your life. Always remember your first love, Jesus; the Love of God remains even in your downfall. The Father has loved you with an Everlasting Love since the beginning of time and will continue to love you, until the end of time. "The steadfast love of the LORD never ceases; His mercies never come to an end" – Lamentations 3:22 [ESV]. There is nothing that you could do to disqualify you from receiving the Love of God, as the scripture tells us in Romans 8:38-39, "And I am convinced that nothing can ever separate us from God's love. Neither death nor life, neither angels nor demons, neither our fears for today nor our worries about tomorrow—not even the powers of hell can separate us from God's love. No power in the sky above or in the earth below—indeed, nothing in all creation will ever be able to separate us from the love of God that is revealed in Christ Jesus our LORD" [NLT]. No matter how far away you've gone and no matter what you have done, understand that His grace still covers you; all you have to do is come back to Jesus and cry out to Him. Repent and He will surely deliver you from any pit that Satan dug for you; "do not rejoice over me, O my enemy. Though I fall I will rise; though I dwell in darkness, the LORD is a light for me" – Micah 7:8 [NASB].

As descendants of Adam and Eve, sin has been passed down in our nature because of their disobedience which then led to the fall of mankind; "For all have sinned and fall short of the glory of God" – Romans 3:23 [NKJV]. Though we fall short, God's love and grace still abound; it is for this very reason that Jesus came to die for us on the cross and reconcile us back to God; "For God so loved the world, that he gave His only begotten son, that whoever believes in Him should not perish but have everlasting life" – John 3:16 [NKJV].

Just as in the Parable of the Prodigal Son [Luke 15:11-32], where the father was waiting for his child to return home; in the same way, even though we are born sinners and live a life of sin, God waits for every one of us – His children – to return home.

There came a point in time where the lost son began to re-evaluate his life and question how he got to such a low point; "When he came to his senses, he said, 'How many of my father's hired servants have food to spare, and here I am starving to death!'" – Luke 15:17 [NIV]. My prayer for you is that, though you may fall, may you never fall so unrecognisably far away from God that you give up on Him because He will *never* give up on you; but rather, always rely on Him, get back up and keep walking with Him. However, if you ever find yourself in that position – backslidden, perhaps that's where you are at now – just know that God's arm is not too short to pull you out of your mess and save you [Isaiah 59:1]. Just as the lost son came to his senses, you must do the same and re-evaluate. Sometimes, all that entails, is to acknowledge your wrong doings, put your pride aside and go back to your Father in heaven – the God of abundance Who is merciful, faithful, just, willing and ready to forgive you of your sins [1 John 1:19].

You don't have to struggle all by yourself like a child without parents or guardians. In your darkest times, call upon the LORD. Whether all your university friends leave you, your real family abandons you and you think you're all alone, or the stress from assignments overwhelms you to the point you feel like giving up; these examples demonstrate some perfect moments in which you can choose to go back to God – when you are weary and have come to the end of yourself. Don't try to fix yourself first – go to Him first. No matter how broken you are, He can fix and heal you. Just like the father in the story was happy to welcome his son back home, with open arms, God also rejoices when you come back home to Him; "But the father said to his servants, 'Bring quickly the best robe and put it on him, and put a ring on his hand, shoes on his feet, and bring the fattened calf and kill it, and let us eat and celebrate'" – Luke 15:22-23 [ESV]. This is how much God looks forward to your return home. Understand that you are loved by the Father and that there is nothing that can separate you from His love.

Maybe you've tried coming back to God several times, but keep finding yourself running back to sin and repeatedly getting stuck in messy situations; you want to stop but you don't know how? You need to surrender. Come back to your first love – Jesus Christ. Open yourself up to receive His Love; because in doing so, you also open yourself up to receive healing, forgiveness, deliverance, restoration and so much more. Perhaps you're struggling to surrender because you think sin *"tastes better"*? Or perhaps, other people have hurt you in the past, now you have trust issues – to the point you feel like you can't trust God… Let me fill you in on a couple of things; the pleasure or the "sweetness" that sin gives you is only for a moment – the aftertaste is a bitter one; an eternity of perishing in hell, which is totally *not* worth putting your soul on the line for. Secondly, the Bible repeatedly says that God will never leave you, fail you, hurt you or forsake you – He is a loving God. So, don't let the mistakes of those who mishandled your heart push you away from the only One who knows best, how to care for it. As you fully surrender to Him – breaking down the walls you've built in your heart and mind – and allow Him to pour out His love on you, your life will be transformed in a way like no other as you receive it. As you get to understand more and more, just how much He loves you, you lose the appetite for those things of the world, you don't want to do those sinful things anymore and you become hungry for God and His Word. Plus, your eyes are open to the deception behind the *'pleasure'* of sin and to the plans that the enemy had in mind for your downfall and extermination, which motivates you to cut off those destructive behaviours. Surrender starts with repentance; that is, turning away from sin. No matter how much your flesh wants to, you turn away – it's almost like saying, *"Jesus, I choose you over this sin"*. Allow that change of heart to lead you into spending time in His presence; praying, dancing/singing to Him, studying His Word and being still to hear His voice – then you will find yourself falling more and more in love with Him. It is my prayer that, if you haven't experience His love already – for you to encounter His love; or if you did have that encounter, once upon a time – but have found that you have fallen away – I pray that you remember your first love, have a fresh encounter and a deeper revelation of His love so that, you not only fall in love with Him, but *stay* in love with Him and grow in His love each day.

Chapter Seven

BE AN EXAMPLE OF CHRIST IN YOUR UNIVERSITY

I've always heard the saying: "be careful how you live because your life may be the only Bible some people read and you may be the only bit of Jesus that some people see" – and this is so true; some people have never actually read the Bible before and may never get to read it either. As Christians, we're basically walking and talking Bibles to the world! "As long as I am in the world, I am the light of the world" – John 9:5 [ESV]. Moreover, the fact that you're also a young person means that, this light within you is supposed to shine even whilst at university. Despite the worldly standards and views that claim wild, unruly behaviour is the norm for students – it is not the norm for you as a Christian. Know that it is possible to live a righteous life, even in that environment. You should stand firm in your identity in Christ. God strategically placed you in your university for a reason – to shine your light, not for it to become dim or to be put out!

Your lifestyle ought to be like a Bible to unbelievers; so, it's your duty to ensure that – you – the bible they're reading, reflects the life of Christ. You do not always have to speak to people trying to persuade them to come to your church – in some instances, a person may just look at your life and *see* that you're different from the rest of the world; seeing this difference in you will make them want to know the reason behind it – in the end, they find Christ! For example, they may want to know why you're so successful, or the reason behind your smile and why you always remain joyful and positive whilst everyone else is panicking. Remember, "You are the salt of the earth; but if the salt loses its flavour, how shall it be seasoned? It is then good for nothing but to be thrown out and trampled underfoot by men" – Matthew 5:13 [NKJV]. The life that you live could either draw people to the saving knowledge and love of Christ, or push them further from Him. It is your responsibility to positively impact the lives of the people that God has placed in your life – e.g. the people that you sit in lectures with that don't know Christ or that brother/sister in your group assignment that doesn't believe in God. Instead of ignoring people or spending time arguing with them in efforts to prove that God exists, why don't you just let your actions do the talking? Why not let them see the love God in you? "If someone says, "I love God" and hates his brother, he is a liar; for he who does not love his brother whom he has seen, how can he love God whom he has not seen?" – 1 John 4:20 [NKJV]. We are always quick to say we love God whom we have never seen before, yet there are people around us that we need to show love to. The sad truth is that there are even certain people who receive nothing but constant hatred from us! Sometimes we look down on people because of their race or even disability, without remorse; we categorise people and write them off without giving them a chance – that must change and we need to do better. If you claim to be a Christian yet people are unable to see Christ in you, then perhaps a self-evaluation is needed to deal with that big question mark of uncertainty looming over your Christianity. In 1 Corinthians 11:1, Apostle Paul said, "Imitate me, as I also imitate Christ" [NKJV]. Some people may argue that Paul is being boastful in this passage, however, I believe that he is simply and frankly expressing that he is not living a double life. It's so easy to fall into the trap of sugar coating the lifestyle you're living, when you even know deep down inside of you that it's not measuring up to the standard, who is Jesus. Paul didn't beat around the bush to try and prove or justify himself – no one could have argued back because his actions backed up his words and he practiced what he was preaching! So, he was just saying it how it is! He was confident that his lifestyle was reflecting the life of Christ. He was confident that he was being a good reflection of Christ to those around him. This is the level of confidence that we, as Christians should aspire to have; a level where we are certain and have complete confidence in our identity in Christ. How confident are you that you are imitating the image of Christ in your daily life? Do you get defensive when a preacher's sermon – using the Word of God – seems to expose the true intentions and nature of your heart or when a fellow brother/sister in Christ comes to correct you in love about certain things in your life? May the LORD help us all and give us the grace to be able to demonstrate all the fruits of the Holy Spirit so that we may shine our light and be the example of Christ in this dark world.

Chapter Eight

YOU ARE THERE FOR A PURPOSE

There is a reason for every season in our lives. At every point in your life there is a reason why you're there and it is your duty to find out – why you're in that season. Yes, you may have achieved the grades required to get into your first-choice university; however, there is a reason why they didn't accept you and a reason why you had to go to a different university. It's not because you're not smart enough or not good enough, but it's because God has a bigger and better plan and assignment for your life which will be realised at another university. Whatever happens and wherever He leads you to, it is for His glory to be shown. God strategically places you in the right university, not just to get a good degree but also because there are lives that you must impact. Not only will you make an impact on other people's lives, but other people will also have an impact on your life; these are divine appointments. The fact that you meet and cross paths with certain people, is not accidental; even if you think you ended up at a certain university by accident – God had already planned every day of your life before the foundations of the earth were established [Psalm 139:16]. Understand that God knows more than you could ever imagine, plus, He has your best interest at heart – He will not allow you to miss out on those opportunities to impact and be impacted.

No matter what plans we may have, God always has a bigger and better plan for our lives; ""For I know the plans I have for you," declares the LORD, "plans to prosper you and not to harm you, plans to give you hope and future'" – Jeremiah 29:11 [NIV]. Your job as young person following Christ is to be obedient to God and avail yourself to Him for His work because your younger years are the days in which you have more strength and energy to ignite and walk in your fire for God without other demands that come with ageing. Ecclesiastes 12:1 even tells us, "remember your Creator in the days of your youth, before the days of trouble come and the years approach when you will say, "I find no pleasure in them"" [NIV]. As young as you are, this is the time to start allowing yourself to be used by God to achieve His purpose in your life. The younger you are, the fewer commitments you have related to adult life. If you start walking fully with God now – not one foot in, one foot out – and pursuing purpose, it will be easier for you to you to adapt to the changes and responsibilities that come later in life, such as marriage and children. As you grow and do life with Christ, He leads and guides you through those new seasons of life as they come. Don't say, *"I'll do what I want now and become serious about God when I'm older"* ... "Do not boast about tomorrow, for you do not know what a day may bring forth" – Proverbs 27:1 [NKJV]. So many people make plans without God and never actually get to live them. You don't know what tomorrow holds; so, hold fast to the One Who is Constant and Unchanging; let Him to lead you through the days He's planned for you and allow Him to use you; the time is now. Some biblical examples of young people God used mightily are: David who defeated Goliath and the Philistine army while he was still a youth [1 Samuel 17], Daniel and his peers (all young men) who purposed in their hearts not defile themselves with food from the king's table regardless of the life-threatening consequences involved [Daniel 1:8] and Joseph who was sold by his brothers to Egypt as a slave [Genesis 37:12-36].

No matter what the enemy plans against your life; if you partner with and align yourself with God, it is only His Will that will succeed in the end. "No weapon formed against you shall prosper" – Isaiah 54:17 [NKJV]... As Christians, sometimes we get disheartened when we face trials of any kind and ask God, "why me?" – please take note, The LORD did not say that we will not experience any hardship at all, nor did He say that life would be easy; in fact, Jesus said that the world will hate us for they hated Him also [John 15:18]. So, remember, the weapons will form – but rest assured that when they do, they will not succeed or prosper against

The Young Christian at University

you. Joseph faced the weapons that formed against him (when his brothers plotted to kill him – Genesis 37:20) but they did not prosper against him. But rather, in that process came the fulfilment of his purpose! This is why I began by saying; there is a reason for every season! No matter what season we go through; good or bad, God has a purpose and a plan, so it's important to focus on what God's Will is for that season. In every test there is a testimony, for every pain there is a purpose and every broken stage in our lives prepares us for the making (that which is ahead of you).

"How do I find my purpose?" – This is a question that I had been asking myself for a very long time. Surely, God said He knows the purpose for which He created us [Exodus 9:16] – meaning that there is a purpose for every life on earth; yours, mine, your friends, your neighbours… But what we'd most like to know as individuals is what our own purpose is. Many people search high and low trying to discover their purpose; looking in all kinds of self-help books and asking everybody and anybody BUT the Creator of life Himself. One of my brothers came to speak at my university on the topic of *"Purpose"*. A young lady asked him, *"How do you find your purpose?"* to which he responded with this question; *"what phone have you got?"*. The young lady replied, *"I have an iPhone"* and then the brother asked her, *"Would you take your iPhone to a Samsung store to fix it when it's broken? Or if you don't not know how use your Apple product?"* After the young lady replied *"no"* – the brother then explained how this same principle applies to our lives and purpose. Many people are quick to pursue the word of a prophet, pastor, apostle or speaker to find out their purpose and God's direction rather than pursuing the Creator of life Himself and His Word. Just as you would take your iPhone to Apple, the manufacturer – for repairs, usage instructions, spare parts or any queries; this is the same way you need to turn to God concerning your purpose and everything in your life! We wouldn't take our Apple products to Samsung or Nokia stores for troubleshooting purposes, so why then, are we so quick to try and fix or find out about ourselves using other sources but God? Sure, there may be some prophets who could give you some sort of word about your future – but that word should only come as a confirmation of something that God has already told you. So, listen carefully – what is God saying *to you*? What is He revealing *to you* about your life?

I went through a dark period in my life where I was at my lowest point. At that time, I had been suspended from my church because of sleeping with a young lady from there. After this, people left me and some of my friends stopped speaking to me – so in the end, it was just God and me. In that season, I began seeking the LORD more than ever before. I came to Him to repent and was seeking Him for comfort and restoration; I knew there was a void and emptiness in my life that needed to be filled and I came to understand that only He could fill it. It was in that period that I received the vision for this book. "Ask, and it will be given to you; seek, and you will find; knock, and the door will be opened to you" – Matthew 7:7 [NKJV]. Regardless of what I had done and what I had been through, the revelation about this book made me realise that God still wanted to use me. Rest assured that, no matter where you have been and no matter what you have done, God has forgiven you – you just need to receive His forgiveness; if you're struggling to receive it, perhaps you also need to forgive yourself. Once you repent and wholly receive God's forgiveness you can then move on. Yes, you may fall at times, but you must never stay down! Get back up and keep going. God is able to use every negative experience you've been through for His glory – no matter how 'dirty', 'corrupt', 'messed up' or 'unforgivable' you may consider it, whatever the case may be – Your surrender and obedience to His call of purpose on your life will, not only unleash a new level of freedom in your life, but also in the lives of many who will be impacted by your testimony. Don't let the devil make you believe the *lies* that you are 'good for nothing' or disqualified from being used by God; "and they overcame him by the blood of the Lamb and by the word of their testimony" – Revelation 12:11 [NKJV].

Chapter Nine

YOU ARE A LEADER

""… You know that the rulers in this world lord it over their people, and officials flaunt their authority over those under them, but among you it will be different. Whoever wants to be a leader among you must be your servant, and whoever wants to be first among you must be the slave of everyone else."" – Mark 10:42-44 [NLT].

To most of us, being in a position of leadership sounds like an amazing accolade and even inspires many of us to seek and attain such positions so that we can put it on our CVs to impress future employers. However, the position of a leader is not just a glamourous title to decorate your CV or LinkedIn account. Why do you even want to be a leader? Are you looking to be the change that the world needs or are you just hungry for power and influence to promote your own agenda in society? Do you want to be a leader, just so people know that you're the boss or that you are in charge? Are you part of the solution or are you going to contribute to the problem? – The world needs a generation of young people who are going to stand up as honourable leaders who will affect change in society; people with a positive influence, who will also be the role models for the younger generation who are the leaders of tomorrow.

A lot of people claim that they are future leaders, but when *is* this future? And how long of a future is being discussed? – Because leadership is a quality that doesn't just develop overnight. What are you doing today to ensure that you become a good leader tomorrow? Have you prepared yourself physically, mentally, spiritually and emotionally for what is coming? It's very easy for anyone to call themselves a leader, but are you ready to step up to the plate when called upon? First, let's define what it means to be a 'good leader'. A good leader is one that can serve those around him. Jesus is the perfect example of a great leader to look up to. In John 13:3-17, we see Jesus washing and drying the feet of His disciples as a demonstration of how they are to serve one another; just as He served them. Though He was their leader, He humbled Himself to the point of washing their feet as an act of service. Many people have the misconception that being 'at the top' and spewing out commands left, right and centre is what makes a leader; but that is not the case – that example sounds more like dictatorship rather than leadership. But with the example of Jesus, we see that – to lead is it serve. Jesus left this example for us as His followers, to love and serve others as He did. How do you take it when you are given a task to accomplish which seems "low" in ranking? Do you humbly give yourself to help and serve, or do you demand your own way – seeking only to be served or to do the more glamorous looking tasks? Jesus said in Matthew 20:28, "for the Son of Man came not to be served but to serve others and give his life as a ransom for many" [NLT]. So, if God Himself – the Creator of the Universe – humbled Himself so much, to the point of leaving His heavenly home, to be born a man on this earth as Jesus to give his life for us, then how much more do we need to lay our lives down for the sake of others as our act of service?

No matter your age, gender or even ethnic background; nothing can or should stand in the way of what God has ordained for you – you can receive that with all the boldness and enthusiasm within you; however, as much as you speak the part and dress the part of who God is calling you to be, you must also walk in it and most importantly, genuinely be the part – don't put on a façade. As coheirs with Christ, we are not meant to just be seeking titles and 'talking the talk', but rather, walking the walk too, just as Jesus did. Moreover, who you become tomorrow, is a result of who you've taught yourself to be from yesterday; so, discipline is key! "As a man thinketh in his heart, so is he" [Proverbs 23:7]. Clearly, we have learned that being a good leader means to serve – so, if pride or selfishness are issues you deal with in your life; start disciplining yourself by loving others, practicing humility, selflessness and service from today onwards so that you grow and develop into that leader you have been called to be. This is just one example out of many practical steps you could exercise to become all that God says you are.

Renew your mind to think positively and speak positively over your life; never give the enemy room to tell you what you can and cannot do. The enemy can come in all sorts of shapes and forms. Sometimes, it's even the people closest to you that will say the most discouraging things. These are things that you may not want to hear, but it's up to you to choose whether you will let those words bring you down or push you towards growth. Some people may argue that their remarks are simply constructive criticism, as for you – learn to discern which remarks are given in love for your edification and which are just negative for the purpose of discouraging you. Imagine someone was throwing bricks at you, their intention may be to harm or bring you down – but what you can do is, instead of engaging in war with that person, rise above it and use those bricks to build a house! In a similar manner, learn how to use negative comments, almost like fuel to build something positive rather than submitting to defeat; you are more than a conqueror. Once you start advancing in your field, people will always find something to talk about regardless of what you do – whether good or bad. Therefore, it is important to train your mind how to deal with negativity. Even Jesus, our High Priest and Saviour Himself, had to go through testing times. That means, that we as His followers will also be able to get through such testing times. The fact that Jesus was able to live a pure and blameless life amid everything that He was facing and despite the accusations against Him, was so that we could realise and understand that it's possible to live purely and blamelessly like Him, even in the midst of afflictions. Jesus after His season of training, walked in His purpose and began to invade the world with love, fulfilling destiny – but note, the tests and trials didn't just all stop one day – they carried on throughout His ministry, He was just able to discern when to be out and about, and when to retreat to pray and seek God's face.

If we abide in God and His Word abides in us, and we allow Him to mould us into who He wants us to be – then we will grow to become a generation great of leaders, ready to change the world for the better.

Chapter Ten

PRAYER AS A WEAPON

Prayer is means of communication between man and God. It enables you to express your sincere gratitude to Christ for all that He has done for you, as well as seek Him for help. One way that your personal relationship with God can be strengthened is through constant prayer. Not just any kind of prayer, but more specifically, prayer based on the Word of God. God said that His word will never return to Him void and that it will always accomplish the purpose for which He sent it [Isaiah 55:11]. So, when we quote God by His Word, we are agreeing with Him and claiming the promises that He has made to us! – The result? – Prayers answered to the highest calibre; He will do exceeding and abundantly above all that we can ask. "For all of God's promises have been fulfilled in Christ with a resounding "Yes!" And through Christ, our "Amen" (which means "Yes") ascends to God for his glory" – 2 Corinthians 1:20 [NLT].

As God's children, there is no doubt that He wants us to depend on Him with all our hearts; and one way to show God that we are choosing to depend on Him is by offering up prayer to Him. When we pray, we are acknowledging God and letting Him know that we trust in Him, His Power, His Sovereignty to do what He knows is best for us and His Faithfulness to fulfil all His promises; this is why the scripture tells us in Philippians 4:6, "be anxious for nothing, but in everything by prayer and supplication, with thanksgiving, let your requests be made known to God" [NKJV] and He will surely come to your aid. You cannot afford to think you can do life on your own and lean on your own understanding, especially whilst at university. Being away from the parental home, university is the season in life where many people claim they are stepping into "freedom". But the truth of the matter of the fact is, if you do not know yourself – I'm talking about knowing yourself as God knows you, not in the way you *think,* you know yourself – university is a place where you can fall into many of the enemy's traps, as his aim is to steal, kill and destroy [John 10:10], as well as see you derailed in life, far from God's presence – that is not a life of freedom, but bondage. The devil may set you up to fail, but all hope is not lost! Prayer is a weapon that positions you to partner with God, sets you up to win at life and fulfil destiny; so, don't underestimate the power of prayer.

The environment at university is not something to be taken lightly... It wasn't until I came to university that I finally started to understand the bible verse: Ephesians 6:12 which says, "…we do not wrestle against flesh and blood, but against principalities, against powers, against the rulers of the darkness of this age, against spiritual hosts of wickedness in the heavenly places" [NKJV]. In a previous chapter, I mentioned that, these days of your youth are the best time to ignite your fire for God because with aging, comes many other demands and excuses. However, the enemy knows the potential of young people; he knows YOUR potential and his agenda is to squash that greatness placed inside of you by God and prevent it from coming into fruition. The devil can't stand the fact that what God wants to birth through you will change the world – populate heaven, plunder hell empty and ultimately, defeat him and his evil plans. University is like a training ground that prepares you for the real world; please know that, once you're out there, the devil doesn't just suddenly play nice – that's why it's important to learn how to deal with him now as early as you can. Those world-changing, kingdom dreams and visions that God has given you may appear small to begin with, but they are part of a much bigger picture. Unfortunately, the devil would rather stop you in your tracks towards destiny as soon as possible – and it just so happens that university provides extremely favourable conditions for the enemy's plans to take course. But don't worry, all hope is not lost! You must learn to fight; I'm not talking about physically, but spiritually.

From the previous scripture, our eyes are opened to the fact that the battle we are in is not a physical one but a spiritual one. Just in case you didn't know – certain things that you're experiencing in your life in the physical realm are not random or by chance, but are because of constant attacks occurring against you in the spiritual realm. On numerous occasions, I've met and spoken to people in university who have mind blowing dreams and visions but haven't even done anything with those ideas yet; they are still sitting on them – that is called stagnancy. The spirit of stagnancy is just one of many other spirits that people allow to wreak havoc in their lives just by simply taking a backseat in their relationship with God and slipping into prayerlessness. As a result, many go down the wrong path or lose themselves completely; these are occurrences which can easily be avoided by using the power of prayer. Now the Bible tells us in 2 Corinthians 10:3-4, "For though we walk in the flesh, we do not war according to the flesh. For the weapons of our warfare are not carnal but mighty in God for pulling down strongholds" [NKJV]. Please understand, you cannot fight spiritual battles in a fleshly manner! The devil will send all sorts of attacks your way, but trying to kick, punch or shout at him will not do anything; God has given you divine weapons to defeat him and prayer is one of those weapons. Prayer must be an extremely powerful weapon because in 1 Thessalonians 5:17, Apostle Paul admonishes us to "pray without ceasing" [NKJV]. The Greek for this scripture translates to, "pray without intermission" – that means, there is no room for prayerlessness and there is a reason why Paul makes this very important point. It's because the enemy is constantly prowling around like a roaring lion, looking for someone to devour [1 Peter 5:8] – and you don't want that to be you; therefore, you can't afford – not to pray! The devil should not be able to catch you off guard, remaining prayerful will ensure that he doesn't. If you want to defeat him, his plans and devices, then you must make sure that prayer is a frequently used weapon from the divine arsenal that God has given you.

    The kingdom of darkness is on a mission to try fill up hell and prevent God's Kingdom of Light from invading the earth – they do not sleep on us, so we cannot afford to sleep on them. Don't get me wrong – you don't have to lose sleep worrying and panicking over what the enemy and his agents are plotting – not at all. What you must be able to do, is know how to stand against the devil in this spiritual war. We have already established that God has given us divine weapons for battle, prayer being one of them. But a warrior doesn't just go into battle unshielded and exposed;

The Young Christian at University

a prudent warrior enters the battlefield with the appropriate protection to complement and maximise the efficacy of his weapons. As warriors in God's army, that protection He has provided us with is a whole set of armour – fully illustrated in Ephesians 6:13-17; "Therefore, put on every piece of God's armour so you will be able to resist the enemy in the time of evil. Then after the battle you will still be standing firm. Stand your ground, putting on the belt of truth and the body armour of God's righteousness. For shoes, put on the peace that comes from the Good News so that you will be fully prepared. In addition to all of these, hold up the shield of faith to stop the fiery arrows of the devil. Put on salvation as your helmet, and take the sword of the Spirit, which is the word of God" [NLT].

As a warrior in God's army, you need to put on the belt of truth because the devil – the father of lies [John 8:44] – is running rampant in the world with mass deception. God's standard is truth; therefore, if you align yourself with it, your discernment will be fortified and you will always have the upper hand over the enemy.

There is also a need for you to live a righteous life; one that is in right-standing with God. That breastplate of righteousness is a reminder to live right – not enslaved by sin – but according to God's Word, that way the devil will never have a foothold to use you as his own device.

Your feet are to be covered with the Gospel of Peace – *Why?* You may ask – seeing as it is your feet that carry you everywhere, the symbolism of peace on your feet signifies that no matter what circumstance you walk into (whether good or bad) and no matter what kind of people you meet, peace can abound in that place – even in the midst of chaos – because Jesus gives peace that surpasses all understanding [Philippians 4:7], not as the world gives [John 14:27]. As a result, you can live in peace, in the midst of storms and testing times, as well as in love, in harmony and in unity with those around you because of the Power of God's Spirit which destroys the devices of the enemy that try to remove peace and cause divisions and strife.

The shield of faith is an essential piece of armour for a prayer warrior because it quenches every fiery dart of the enemy. An example of one type of fiery dart is 'doubt'. At times, the enemy will attack your prayers with doubt, but you must fight that doubt with faith by holding up your shield! Remember without faith it is impossible to please God. James 1:6-7 says, "But let him ask in faith, with no doubting, for he who doubts is like a wave of the sea driven and tossed by the wind. For let not that man suppose that he will receive anything from the LORD" [NKJV]. The devil knows that if he can make you doubt and diminish your faith in God to nothing – then you will have no faith left to even please God, thus leaving your faithless prayers consequently, unanswered.

When you become saved, you are adopted into the family of God [Ephesians 1:5]. After this point, you become aware of your identity in Christ as well as your inheritance as a child of God. The enemy doesn't want you to know about these things because he knows that, if you know, *who you truly are* – in Christ – then he doesn't stand a chance against you! Therefore, you must put on the helmet of salvation which will guard your mind and block him from gaining access. It keeps the truth of who you are and whose you are securely locked in your mind so that the devil can't tell you otherwise and deceive you into thinking less of yourself than who God says you are.

Last but not least, is the Sword of The Spirit – The Word of God – which is sharper than any double-edged sword [Hebrews 4:12]. There is so much power in God's Word and when you know how to apply and use it; the devil will have no choice but to leave. In Matthew 4:1-11, Jesus was tempted by the devil – but He fought back by speaking The Word alone. Yes, the devil quoted some scripture too; but he didn't have the backing of the Holy Spirit as Jesus did and as you and I have. When you take up the Word by studying it, meditating on it, memorising it and hiding it in your heart, then when you come to use it by speaking it, praying it or declaring it; God will show His Power with the Holy Spirit. So, trust in the LORD and equip yourself with the weapons and armour He has given you that will help you stand against the enemy.

Chapter Eleven

LIVE BY FAITH, NOT BY SIGHT

"Now faith is the substance of things hoped for, the evidence of things not seen" – Hebrews 11:1 [NKJV]. Faith is believing that something exists or has happened before it has come into being. Everything that has ever been created was once just a thought before being spoken into existence. There was a module in my second year of university that I remember being so complex, that most of my peers decided to change modules. While they all changed to do something else, I decided to stay in that module even though it meant sitting in its lectures, two hours every Monday for Six weeks – and I had barely learnt a thing. An important test was fast approaching at the time as well. Honestly, I would always leave the lectures feeling even more confused than I was before I came in. The one thing that kept me on that module and even attending the lectures was God speaking to me. I had this strong conviction telling me, *"Hayford, stay in this module and don't give up because I will give you a testimony"*. So, whenever my friends would ask me about the module, I would always say, *"God is going to give me a testimony"*. I was certain within myself that the LORD had my back and that I was not going to fail the module. After everything was said and done – the confusing lectures, the all-nighters of revision in the library and the final exam – come results day, I found out that, that module gave me my highest grade in my entire second year! With God, nothing is too hard or impossible.

The scripture tells us that, the Word that comes out of God's mouth will not return to Him void, unless it has accomplished what He desires and its purpose [Isaiah 55:11]. There is so much that the LORD has set out for us; He has plans and a purpose for our lives, including our past, present and future – but these things can only come to pass when we put our faith in action; "For we walk by faith not by sight [living our lives in a manner consistent with our confident belief in God's promises]" – 2 Corinthians 5:7 [AMP]. Our faith should drive us to obey God's Word. Look at it this way, every invention starts with a vision, but it takes faith to carry the vision and bring it into fruition. The vision is carried by faith just as a woman carries her unborn child in the womb when she is pregnant – although she cannot see the baby in her womb, she believes and has faith that after 9 months she will have a new bundle of joy. Therefore, she puts measures in place by changing her lifestyle to make sure that the baby is growing as healthily as possible; she may stop smoking or drinking and start eating healthier and relaxing more instead of succumbing to stressful situations. The point is, she takes the necessary action to protect that baby up to birth. When women don't take care of themselves during pregnancy, there runs the risk of complications within the baby – and even miscarriage at times. So, protect your vision with faith. When I relate this back to my situation, the vision I had of passing the module, was carried by my faith which encouraged me to put measures into place so that I could see that success come into fruition. Even though the content was difficult and the lectures confusing, faith encouraged me to keep attending the lectures and keep studying. You know, faith without works is dead [James 2:14-26]. When we don't protect our vision with faith and works, there runs the risk of that idea falling through – such as with the miscarriage or complications at birth in pregnancy. Yes, you may be trusting in God for something, but if you don't put in the action to prove that you're truly believing in God for that thing to come to pass, then it shows a lack of faith. You must partner with God and do your part. God cannot work with you, if you do not have complete faith in Him, the Word tells us in Hebrews 11:6, "… without faith it is impossible to please God, because anyone who comes to Him must believe that He exists and that He rewards those who earnestly seek Him" [NIV].

Chapter Twelve

IT'S ONLY BY HIS GRACE

Grace is defined as "unmerited favour". A popular acronym for GRACE is: 'God's. Riches. At. Christ's. Expense'. "Therefore, as it is written: "Let the one who boasts boast in the LORD"" – 1 Corinthians 1:31 [NIV].

You know those times when it seems like all odds are against you, yet you still manage to obtain a 1st or a 2:1 in your studies? For example, when you go into an exam having revised only two or three topics as opposed to the whole module; yet, you find that what came up in the exam paper was exactly what you had covered? Know that, that was not because of your own, strength, wisdom, knowledge or power – but it was because of the LORD who saw you through! "… 'Not by might nor by power but by My Spirit,' Says the LORD of hosts" – Zechariah 4:6 [NKJV]. In other instances, stress and depression may consume your peers but because you have Christ, when the tough times come, God's grace always rescues you! "Many are the afflictions of the righteous, but the LORD delivers him out of them all" – Psalm 34:19 [ESV]. How about the times when your fridge is empty and your student finance has run out? If you work, your next pay day may be a couple of weeks away or you may even be jobless – you don't even know what you'll eat today, let alone tomorrow… Worry may begin to creep in, but in the nick of time, God shows up! You just find that one aunty or friend comes and blesses you with food so that you still have something to eat and drink – that is the doing of Jehovah Jireh Who provides for you! Not luck, nor chance; never forget it. "The LORD's blessing brings wealth, and no sorrow comes with it" – Proverbs 10:22 [NCV] – despite the hurdles you may face at university, once you finish, you'll eventually come to realise that *'no sorrow'* came with it because every situation had a lesson in it which was a blessing in disguise.

As you go through your university journey, please know that your success is found in Christ, not in the materialistic worldly view of success. With our human eyes, success will look different for each person so don't compare your journey with anyone else's journey; the important thing is to always remember that "all things work together for good to those who love God, to those who are called according to His purpose", as the scripture tells us in Romans 8:28 [NKJV]. So, yes, you are at university for a purpose; no, it's not going to be smooth sailing throughout – however, God's grace will carry and guide you through the wonderful plan He has for your life – you just need to trust Him, believe in Him and partner with Him. Also, be sure to make known the name of the God who blesses you in the good times and helps you in the difficult times because you couldn't do it on your own and come out sane on the other side! Acknowledging and praising God through everything will help establish a sound mind in you. When things go well in your life, it's very easy to get big-headed, praise your own efforts and feel self-sufficient; this is very dangerous because should there be a turn of events, your composure can very easily be knocked, thus hindering you from progressing and moving forward in life. So, understand that you are not sufficient in yourself but in Christ. There is a common saying that states, "God helps those who help themselves", but this is not actually biblical. God tells us in 2 Corinthians 12:9, "My grace is sufficient for you, for my power is made perfect in weakness" [ESV] – So, in actual fact, God helps those who admit they *can't* help themselves and confess that they need Him! If you boast more gladly in your weaknesses and in the LORD rather than in your own strength, be prepared to see Him show up and move mightily in your life! So, praise Him when things go well; this will remove pride and cultivate humility – "God resists the proud, but gives grace to the humble" – James 4:6 [NKJV]. I'm very sure you don't want God to resist you... Furthermore, praise God when things are not going well because your praise gives birth to breakthrough and establishes peace of mind, after all, true peace only comes from God, not from anything the world can offer you [John 14:27].

It is so important that you share the testimonies of what God has done for you so that others may also believe and come to the saving knowledge of our LORD, Jesus Christ. The devil is running rampant in so many people's lives but your testimony may be the key to someone else's breakthrough when they hear about how – through Christ – you defeated the enemy in different situations in your own life; "… they overcame and conquered him because of the blood of the Lamb and because of the word of their testimony…" – Revelation 12:11 [AMP]. It's literally a matter of life and death, so don't be shy or scared to share what Jesus has done for you so that others can also be set free – "For whoever is ashamed [here and now] of Me and My words, the Son of Man will be ashamed of him when He comes in His glory and the glory of the [heavenly] Father and of the holy angels" – Luke 9:26 [AMP].

Understand that it is God who gives and it is Him who can also take away [Job 1:21]. The gifts you possess and the ability to overcome 3 or 4 years of studies is not something to be taken for granted. There are so many people in the world who don't have access to education and could only wish to be in your position, studying the course of their dreams but are unable to do so for several reasons. Moreover, some people are privileged enough to make it to university; however, not everyone is able to make it through and complete all those years. Therefore, let us humble ourselves before the LORD and give Him all the praises that are due, to His name because it's only by His grace that we live – remember that when praises go up, His glory comes down.

Chapter Thirteen

STUDY TO SHOW YOURSELF APPROVED

The main reason you go to university is to study and obtain a degree. After your relationship with God, your degree is a priority that follows closely behind whilst you're at university and must be taken with all seriousness. This means pushing yourself to work hard, at the best of your ability in class as well as attending tutorials & seminars, participating in group work, being organised and revising – all with excellency. After all, the word of God tells us in Colossians 3:23, "whatever you do, do it enthusiastically, as something done for the LORD and not for men" [HCSB]. However, it's common among many students to skip lectures, leave deadlines until the last minute and revise the night before an exam that they've known about for months. Not to mention, taking more breaks than getting actual work done during study sessions! Then, when all the work has piled up and the stress of coursework or exams starts to engulf us; that's when we find it convenient to seek God for help and declare that He is in control. Yes, He is indeed in control but we should also do our part! God will grant you the wisdom and grace to understand the work you have to do but He's not going to type it up for you. God takes care of everything behind the scenes like leading you to the best study materials/resources and touching the hearts of your teachers and examiners to give you favour when marking your work, but you have to do your part too; you must put in the effort - you don't want the favour that God has stored up for you to go to waste, do you?

Genesis 28:10 onwards, speaks about how God met Jacob at the point of His need after he ran away from His family home when his brother Esau wanted to kill him. A common prayer point amongst Christians is, "God, please meet me at the point of my need". This phrase suggests that, in the process of doing something, working towards something or just simply living your life, there came a moment in time when you could no longer carry on but came in need of divine intervention. Much emphasis is often put on the word *"need"*, forgetting that one must first get to a *"point"* to be helped – but have you even started the work, the research, the planning etc.? What effort are you putting in towards the destination you have in mind? Being in need, is the best time to exercise faith. However, understand that faith without works is dead [James 2:14-26]. If I am constantly sleeping or out having fun and socialising whilst my work remains undone, when the deadline now comes, I will expect God to "meet me at the point of my need" – but if I never put in the effort, in the first place then where is that "point"? "At the point of your need" means that you must move and work towards something and not be stagnant. When you fall short, He will pick you up and when you are tired, He will be your strength. One of my favourite scriptures is Proverbs 3:6, I particularly like The Living Bible [TLB] version which says, "in everything you do, put God first, and he will direct you and CROWN YOUR EFFORTS WITH SUCCESS". When you put God first in everything you do – for example with your studies – with the scriptural work ethic; working as though unto Him and not for human masters, being a good steward of the degree He has given you the opportunity to study and being diligent and faithful with what He sets before you, then rest assured that as you put in the work to match your faith, when you do arrive at that point of need, He will surely intervene and crown your efforts with success!

Apostle Paul said to his son in the faith, Timothy, "study to shew thyself approved..." - 2 Timothy 2:15 [KJV]. As a university student, this principle can also be applied whilst you study because in, one way or another, your knowledge will be tested. Moreover, as Christians, we need to operate in God's Spirit if Excellence! People in the world should be able to see how you enjoy and excel in life, regardless of the hurdles and struggles you face; not because of your own power or might, but because of Jesus in your life. So, make sure you work hard towards the goal in mind, it won't always be easy but with the grace of God, you will overcome university – university will not kill you in Jesus' name!

21-Day Devotional

Having gained some insight and understanding about how to overcome some of the challenges at university, you can now put into practice the habit of studying the word by taking part in this 21-day devotional. Spending time with God is an essential part of your spiritual growth and the key to surviving university as a Christian. I suggest you set apart a specific time and place to meet with God every day. Also, devote a minimum of at least 10 or 15 minutes of your time for the next 21 days to develop this habit. As you get more disciplined in retreating to your secret place, you will find that you will begin to spend more and more time with God. Make sure you're not distracted by anything or anyone, just allow God to reveal mysteries to you through His Word. Even as you pray, don't forget to leave moments of peace and quietness so that you can hear God speak – that way you will learn to hear His voice…

> "Call to Me, and I will answer you, and show you great
> and mighty things, which you do not know"
> – Jeremiah 33:3 [NKJV].

If possible, try and do your devotions every morning before stepping out of the house; then as you go about your day, meditate on that Word and be mindful of what God is saying to you. Staying in constant communication with your Heavenly Father throughout the day will give you the strength, power and wisdom needed to overcome all the challenges of the day.

DAY 1

RENEW YOUR MIND

"Do not conform to the pattern of this world, but be transformed by the renewing of your mind..."
– Romans 12:2 [NKJV].

The mind is a set of faculties which includes; consciousness, perception, thinking, judgment and memory. It is the control centre which regulates your feelings and influences your actions. Every decision you make is because of a series of thoughts that take place in the mind before the action is performed.

Do not be influenced by the world's way of thinking – society's trap that tries to fit everybody into one box. You are under no obligation to look/dress a certain way or participate in certain activities just because they are perceived as the "norm" for students in the university environment.

Firstly, understand that the world's standards do not align with God's standards. The world's way of thinking focuses on fleshly things, but you need to set your mind on things of above [Colossians 3:2] and understand that as a child of God, you have been given the mind of Christ [1 Corinthians 2:16]. So, on all occasions, ask yourself; "What Would Jesus Do? (WWJD?)" … "Would Jesus say that?" … "Would Jesus think this way?" etc. Renew your mind to think on "what is true, and honourable, and right, and pure, and lovely, and admirable. Think about things that are excellent and worthy of praise" – Philippians 4:8 [NLT]. You do this by meditating on truth, which is The Word of God and by listening to the Holy Spirit.

Meditating on the Word will renew your mind regarding all aspects of your life – from your identity, how to stop sinning and how to treat others, to thinking like Christ, making the right decisions and realising your potential so that you can walk boldly and confidently in your purpose – plus so much more! For example, if being in the world as led you to believe the *lies* that make you think that you are *'ugly'*, *'useless'*, *'not good enough'*, or *'unloved'*, etc., God's Word will reveal to you that you are *'fearfully and wonderfully made'* [Psalm 139:14], *'you were bought with a price'* [1 Corinthians 6:20], you are *'the apple of God's eye'* [Zechariah 2:8] and so much more!

DAY 2

SPEAK INTO EXISTENCE

"Death and life are in the power of the tongue, and those who love it and indulge it will eat its fruit and bear the consequences of their words"
– Proverbs 18:21 [AMP].

The same tongue that you use for building up and inspiration can also be used for tearing down and destruction. Train yourself to speak positive words that will edify you and those around you. This scripture reveals that your words bear fruit; what kind of fruit are your words producing? If you are constantly spewing negativity from your mouth, don't be surprised if you're constantly experiencing negative manifestations in your life. Choose your words wisely and be careful about what you speak upon your life because it will become a reality – so, speak positivity, speak life and speak God's Word of Truth always.

When we look at the story of creation in Genesis, we see how God spoke things into existence. The same Power that God used to speak creation into being lives inside of you! In Genesis 1:3, "… God said, "Let there be light"; and there was light" [NKJV]; He spoke and it came to pass, because you are made in His likeness, you too can speak and see things come to pass. In Mark 11:22-24, Jesus said: ""Have faith in God. For assuredly, I say to you, whoever says to this mountain, 'Be removed and be cast into the sea,' and does not doubt in his heart, but believes that those things he says will be done, he will have whatever he says. 24 Therefore

I say to you, whatever things you ask when you pray, believe that you receive *them,* and you will have *them*"" [NKJV]. So, that business you've always dreamed about, those grades you want to achieve, good health, financial freedom, that family member that isn't saved, etc., don't just stay silent! Start calling these things into existence and trusting in God; moreover, start walking and thanking Him like you've already received it!

The power you possess in your tongue also enables you to remind every demon in hell of who you are, Who you belong to and the Power and authority that He gave to you. The scripture helps us understand that, God has not given us the spirit of fear or timidity but the spirit of love, power and of a sound mind [2 Timothy 1:7]. The enemy has *no* power over us; we – as children of the Most High God – we have the upper hand over him! Unfortunately, we sometimes fall into the trap of speaking destructive words into our lives because of the deceitful thoughts and *lies* that he deposits in our minds. Why claim that you're "shy", "scared", "idiotic", "broke", "worthless etc., when the Bible says the exact opposite of these things? The devil knows that if he can provoke you to speak negative into your life, you will be making his job of bringing you down much easier; don't partner with the devil against your own life and against the lives of those around you!

Matthew 12:36 says, "on the day of judgment people will have to give an accounting for every careless or useless word they speak" [AMP]. How carefully then, must we consider each word we say? Whether it be about our own lives, the lives of those around us or even the city we live in, our workplace, our boss and work colleagues, the school we attend and the world in general – we must always speak life. Sometimes we even make jokes about certain things, thinking they're funny – but not knowing how much of an indelible bad mark it's left in someone's life. Brethren, let us be cautious of what we say at all times. May our words always make a positive impact in people's lives and may we learn to always encourage one another with our words rather that bringing each other down. Let us form the best future with our words; a future that is in alignment with God's perfect plan.

Day 3

SPEND TIME WITH THE LORD

"Like newborn babies, crave pure spiritual milk, so that by it you may grow up in your salvation"
– 1 Peter 2:2 [NIV].

A strong relationship with God is one of the major keys to surviving in the university environment. You strengthen your relationship with God by getting to know Him. You get to know Him by reading The Word because God is in His word; so much about His nature, likes, dislikes and more, are revealed there.

Many people love to tweet a scripture here and quote a scripture there, bringing up God's name in different conversation – but how many people can live out the scripture and apply it to their lives? Everybody loves the scriptures that deploy blessings, favour and provision – we are very quick to decree, declare, claim and receive them too! But how about the scriptures that call for holiness, obedience, forgiving others and turning away from sin? "Your word I have treasured and stored in my heart, that I may not sin against You" – Psalm 119:11 [AMP]. If the word of the LORD is in your heart, you will live it and its fruits will be evident in your life. As You spend time with God, you get to know Him not just as a Blesser, but also as a Father, a Friend and so much more; you also get to know what breaks His heart, His desires, what He requires of you and how to hear His voice.

Furthermore, if you spend time with God, He will order your steps and direct you in the way you should go. "The LORD makes firm the steps of the one who delights in Him" – Psalm 37:23 [NIV]. This includes revelation of your purpose, revelation of destiny helpers and what company to keep, direction into the perfect job for you, choosing a spouse, business ideas etc., – everything concerning your life! You were not made to walk around lost; aimless, clueless and confused. So, make sure you spend time studying the scripture, meditating on the Word and praying – not as part of your "to-do list" – but to genuinely connect with God. Facing God in prayer daily gives you the strength to face the world and the enablement to overcome the trials and the temptations of your surroundings. There's a popular saying that states: "he who kneels before God can stand before anyone".

Every season has its blessings as well as its lessons. You won't know what God is doing or what the enemy is planning against you unless you spend time seeking God. As a child of God, the Holy Spirit Who lives inside of you, is there to teach you and help you understand the Word – so pay attention to what He may be saying to you. Spending time with God is not about reading chapter after chapter and saying lengthy prayers with big words. Connecting with Him is key. You can connect with Him on a deeper, more intimate level by praying sincere prayers from the bottom of your heart, just converse with God – you don't have to prove your ability to pray by using large words and longwinded ramblings. Don't over think it, just relax in His presence. You don't have to read the whole Bible overnight either – sometimes the Holy Spirit will draw you to a specific portion of the Bible to read over and over again until you catch the revelation He's leading you to. It may be the same one chapter or the same few verses over a period of one day, or even one week! Just ask Him what it is He wants you to learn. Another thing is to be still and stay silent in God's presence so that you can hear Him speak. A conversation is a two-way affair; yet a lot of the time when we spend time with God we do most of the talking and then finish up without even giving him a chance to speak like He has nothing to say; yet He has so much to say! Write down whatever He speaks to you. And most importantly, obey! Time spent with God is supposed to transform you; you shouldn't stay the same. Be intentional about applying into your life, what He teaches and commands you to do. "If you love me, you will keep my commandments" – John 14:15 [ESV].

Day 4

WHO AM I?

"He came to His own people, and even they rejected Him. But to all who believed Him and accepted Him, he gave the right to become children of God"
– John 1:11-12 [NLT].

It is important to understand who you are so that you don't go through university trying to live up to people's expectations. You must know who you are in Christ; who does God say you are? "But you are a chosen generation, a royal priesthood, a holy nation, His own special people, that you may proclaim the praises of Him who called you out of darkness into His marvellous light" – 1 Peter 2:9 [NKJV]. You cannot go through university living like everyone else still in the world because you became a new creation when you died to your old nature and came to the LORD. You have been purchased by the blood of Jesus. You are a coheir with Christ. You carry the DNA of God Himself; therefore, you must live accordingly – you can't be living in a way which is contrary to the Word of God. "Those who have been born into God's family do not make a practice of sinning, because God's life is in them. So, they can't keep on sinning, because they are children of God" – 1 John 3:9 [NLT].

God has called you into a life of greatness, so you must walk in it as Christ did. Jesus only did what He saw His Father doing [John 5:19] – He wasn't conforming to the patterns of the world and doing what everyone else was doing because He knew Who He was as the Son of God. Now, God has given you the right to also be His child; Jesus has set the standard for you to imitate. "Imitate God, therefore, in everything you do, because you are His dear children" – Ephesians 5:1 [NLT].

You have been set apart to be a light in this dark world and affect change in it – but if you don't know your true identity, you will just blend into the darkness instead. When you *know* who you are, you will know what sort of activities to take part in and stay away from, you will know which places to go and where not to go, you will know what sort of conversations to engage in and shut down, you will know how to stand firm and not be swayed by peer pressure. You will not compromise. Do you know who you are? Does your life reflect who God says you are? Get to know yourself by seeking Him so that you do not lose yourself amongst the crowd.

Day 5

JUST LET GO!

*"...I focus on this one thing:
Forgetting the past and looking forward to what lies ahead"*
– Philippians 3:13 [NLT].

There's a popular saying that states, "yesterday is history, tomorrow is a mystery and today is a gift; hence why it's called the 'present'". You cannot change the events of yesterday but you can change the outcome of tomorrow by choosing to do something today. What has happened has already passed aside from a few lessons possibly learned, it can't add value to your life now; however, you can take advantage of the opportunities presented to you today to create value for your tomorrow.

Forgive whoever has wronged you in the past. Set your heart, your mind and your body at peace by letting go of the things and the hurt caused by people which has held you back and had you bound. Set yourself free from the miseries of yesterday and look to the victory of tomorrow. Do not let your past control and get in the way of your future because the glory of the latter shall be greater than the former [Haggai 2:9]. Understand that what lies ahead of you is far greater than what you've been through.

Until you overcome certain situations and past hurts in your life, it will be hard to move on to the next level that God wants to take you to. You can delay your own destiny just because you are still hanging on to some bitterness, anger, resentment, jealousy or any other toxic emotion against others that the LORD told you to let go of a long time ago. There is power in forgiveness and letting go. When you forgive those who have wronged you, your mind and your heart are set at peace. You overcome all those things that temporarily held you; the things that you never thought you could be set free from, but with Christ all things are possible. The book of Ecclesiastes tells us about times and seasons of life; there is an appointed time for everything so don't allow certain situations to keep you stagnant – you must constantly be growing in your relationship with God and making progress in your purpose.

God is the true mender of broken hearts, whatever is on your heart pour it out to Him. No matter how broken you think you are, God can bind up your wounds [Psalms 147:3], mould you and turn your mourning into rejoicing once again. Do not carry the burden by yourself; just trust God to make all things new. The Bible says that He makes everything beautiful in its time [Ecclesiastes 3:11]. None of your tears have gone to waste, God has seen every tear you have cried [Psalm 56:8] – there is no need to be disheartened because once you hand everything over to Him, He turns things around four your good. Your breakthrough is coming. You are about to take back everything that the enemy has stolen from you. All you need to do is 'LET GO and LET GOD' – let Him into the deepest darkest places that you've built up in your heart, surrender to Him so that He can deal with each issue once and for all by destroying it at its root. Let go of trying to help yourself or looking like you have it all together and everything under control; acknowledge that you are weak and that you need Him – let the LORD be your strength. Make that decision that allows Jesus to be the driver while you are the passenger – let Him steer your life in the right direction.

Do not delay your own destiny by keeping hold of people, thoughts, memories, emotions and other things that are toxic hindrances to your growth and well-being. Let go and invite God into every situation.

Day 6

FIND FRIENDS WHO BRING OUT THE BEST IN YOU

"Do not be misled: "Bad company corrupts good character""
– 1 Corinthians 15:33 [NIV].

There is so much potential inside of you; probably more than you even realise. Don't be one of those people that are just satisfied with hearing about their potential – take a step further to cultivate it so that your dreams can be realised and your purpose fulfilled! Everyone is unique in their own way, but what makes you different from everyone else is an indication of what the world needs from you – surely, God placed things in you that the world needs as part of its transformation. Therefore, you need to do whatever it takes to release that which God has placed in you. Now, to reach the world, you are going to have to come out of your comfort zone because nothing great ever came from comfort zones; they are not the best environments conducive for growth. Condition yourself to come out of your comfort zone, train yourself to see things from a different perspective; see the bigger picture. We live in a diverse world; God made all types of people so that we could live in harmony together. However, people get comfortable being around those who look like them or can relate to the same cultural background. Step out of the confinement of your own culture or race and make friends with people from different backgrounds.

A wise man once said that "your network is your net worth". If you never broaden your horizons and get to know different types of people, staying around the same kind of people who never challenge you, may limit you. Try and get to know as many people as possible from your course and outside of your course from societies that you wouldn't immediately think to get involved in. I see a lot of segregation at some universities where people don't exactly mix, yet it's so important to do so as we can learn a lot from others. Find friends who are driven to succeed and work on bettering themselves and their gifts so that, that same zeal can rub off on you too. Find friends who care about your development and care enough to check on your progress. Finishing this book was partly because of the friends I kept at university; particularly in my final year. I found brothers and sisters who would hold me accountable for not doing what I'm supposed to be doing. Although such friends could appear to be tough on you sometimes, it is for your best interest and the result is always great. Learn to appreciate such friends; but also, be this type of friend too. Most importantly, find a core group of Christian friends so that you can sharpen one another as iron does [Proverbs 27:17] – friends who not only care about earthly success, but those that keep their minds on things of above. Friends you can pray with, friends you can study the Word with, friends who push you closer to God rather than pulling you away from Him. Also ask yourself if you are this kind of friend too.

Don't waste three or four valuable years, focused on having friends who just want to have fun or send you down the wrong path. Find ambitious friends that can motivate, support and encourage so that you can all do these for one another. Your abilities may differ but success is for all if you are willing to put in the work. Where possible, find a mentor to guide you with the vision and help you develop certain characteristics needed for your chosen field. You should never come out of University the same or worse than you came in. What company do you keep? Do they push you towards the will of God and achieving your goals or do they drive you away from God?

DAY 7

SHOW LOVE TO EVERYONE

"Let everything you do be done in love [motivated and inspired by God's love for us]"
– 1 Corinthians 16:14 [AMP].

When you think about just how much God loves you; in the way that He demonstrated His love with the sacrifice of His Son for our sins even when we were still sinners, running from Him – it makes you realise that you don't really have an excuse or a valid reason for not loving other people. You must show love to everybody; your friends, lecturers and colleagues. You must demonstrate the love of God to whoever you come into contact with, even if they hate you and treat you badly – you love them and treat them nicely. It's not your job to retaliate or fight back with hate because the LORD will fight your battles [Exodus 14:14]. Just never repay evil with evil but rather with blessings [1 Peter 3:9], keep a clear conscious and do not harbour bitterness in your heart. Bitterness will destroy you more than it does the other person. Take that bitterness to the foot of the cross and ask the LORD for a deeper encounter and understanding of His love so that you may also learn how to love.

Do not treat people with hostility or with love? You need to be careful how you speak to everyone to prevent any problems in future; "Don't forget to show hospitality to strangers, for some who have done this have entertained angels without realizing it!" – Hebrews 13:2 [NLT]. Let people glorify your Father in heaven because of your act of kindness towards them. Show the love of God to believers and unbelievers. A person could decide to follow you to church based on how you've treated them and they can also decide not to have any associations with the church; more importantly, your actions either lead them to Christ or away from Him.

"Love is patient and kind. Love is not jealous or boastful or proud or rude. It does not demand its own way. It is not irritable, and it keeps no record of being wronged" – 1 Corinthians 13:4-5 [NLT]. If we are truly the followers and examples of Christ, let us learn to love our neighbours like ourselves [Mark 12:31], for this is what the Father has commanded us to do. Let us love one another even as Christ has loved us.

Day 8

THE WORLD NEEDS YOUR GIFTS

"For that is what the LORD has commanded us, saying, 'I have placed You as a light for the Gentiles, so that You may bring [the message of eternal] salvation to the end of the earth.'"
– Acts 13:47 [AMP].

Every one of us has several gifts that God has given us. These gifts can be seen even in the smallest things we do on a daily basis; however, not everyone has comprehended the gifts they possess – yet, some of those gifts and talents have the ability to make an impact on a global scale. Some people haven't yet realised the potential inside of them and so, see themselves as less than how God sees them. How do you see yourself? Are you aware of the greatness that God has placed in you? Perhaps you often talk down upon yourself; yet, people around you – or even those who hardly know you – often speak highly of you because they can see more in you than you see in yourself.

"Then the LORD asked him, "What is that in your hand?" – "A shepherd's staff," Moses replied" – Exodus 4:2 [NLT]. Whatever God has placed in your hand – in your life – is the same thing He will use to impact this world. Moses had the staff in his hands and that was the tool he used help save the people of Israel; What gifts do *you* have at hand in your toolbelt? God is going to use your gifts to save, to redeem, to heal and to restore His people back to Him. However, this can only happen if you avail yourself to be used as a vessel. God is a gentleman, so He doesn't force you to do anything. I have come to understand that Power in the Kingdom is not based on ability but availability. Don't even worry or think about "not being good enough", that is a lie – as long as you make yourself ready and available to do the will of God, He will use you in a mighty way through His Holy Spirit. Before Jesus ascended back to heaven, He even said, "Very truly I tell you, whoever believes in me will do the works I have been doing, and they will do even greater things than these" – John 14:12 [NIV]. Are you ready to be used by God? Are you ready to represent Him here on earth? Do you know what your gifts are? Perhaps you know a few or don't know any at all – or you may have identified a few but you're not 100% aware of what it is God wants you to do with those gifts and talents. Spend time seeking the LORD as part of your identity search, as you get to know Him more, you get to know yourself more and He will reveal to you, your purpose and what He's called you to do. Ultimately, whatever He calls you to do will be for His glory and for the advancement of His Kingdom. And God is a God of Excellence, so once you've identified the gifts and areas He wants you to focus on, spend time perfecting those gifts so that you use them well! Look at these scriptures associated with your gifts:

"Do you see a man skilful and experienced in his work? He will stand [in honour] before kings; He will not stand before obscure men" – Proverbs 22:29 [AMP].

"A man's gift makes room for him, and brings him before great men" – Proverbs 18:16 [NKJV].

"You are the light of the world. A city that is set on a hill cannot be hidden. Nor do they light a lamp and put it under a basket, but on a lampstand, and it gives light to all who are in the house. Let your light so shine before men, that they may see your good works and glorify your Father in heaven" – Matthew 5:14-16 [NKJV].

God must get all the glory! Because of this, He will not do things on a small scale. Work on your gifts and put them into practice. As you do so, you begin to realise that He placed them in you for a reason far beyond yourself. Be careful; they are not just for money and fame as some people get so easily caught up in! But they are for bringing light to those who are in darkness world over, in turn hell is plundered empty and God is glorified! A lot of the time the devil will discourage you from using your gifts because he knows the potential you possess; so, don't give in.

Day 9

TAKE THE "RISK"

*"Trust in the LORD with all your heart, and
lean not on your own understanding"
– Proverbs 3:5 [NKJV].*

There are levels of "risks" that everyone must take at different stages in life to get to where they want to be in future. Some risks may seem bigger than others but the fact remains that, regardless of what your purpose is, what idea you have, what plans you've got in place; you will always have to make the decision to jump from one level up to the next level to get to that next stage in your life.

Thinking about taking a risk might sound scary – so why don't we look at it in a different way? Look at as having faith and trusting in God; taking a leap of faith. For me, writing this book was a jump I had to take as I'm in the process of fulfilling purpose. Having just finished university, I could have just gone straight into a graduate job as everyone would expect a graduate to do after graduation. But, I know God had other plans. He gave me the vision for this book and I had the strong conviction to finish it so, I decided to obey Him. People could have told me to finish the book whilst in a graduate job – if I had done that, it may have taken another few years before it was done! The thing is, when God leads you, He will give you specific instructions and hold your hand through out. You just need to have faith enough, to trust that what He's asking of you will work out exactly how He said it would. The thing is, if He is a Constant, Never Failing, Never Changing, Faithful God – then surely there is no risk in Him, right? – He leads you in a specific direction or to do a specific thing because He knows that it *will* work out for your good! The whole journey will not be smooth and easy but you can rest assured that it will work out; His word doesn't return to Him void – He doesn't make empty promises. I guess the idea that it is a "risk" comes about because perhaps fear, anxiety and doubt creep in from somewhere. But God has not given you a spirit of fear but of power, of love and of a sound mind [2 Timothy 1:7].

So, take that leap of faith! Pursue your purpose with boldness and all confidence in the LORD that, even if you fall – you know He will catch you. Even if you make a mistake – you know that He will redeem you. Falling is part of the process because it helps you learn lessons, so no part of your journey of process is in vain or ever wasted. Just know that if you stay where you are, you cannot progress. You can't be doing the same things over and over again – e.g. making excuses, procrastination, letting fear stop you – and expect something different to happen or receive a breakthrough out of that. If you want to change the output, you must change your input. Jump… right out of your comfort zone and do something extraordinary. We've already touched briefly on your 'potential' in a previous devotional. By now your mind should be renewed to know that there is so much that God has placed in you waiting to be released. So, step into a new world that is not known to you and a new way of thinking that trusts God without borders, where risk taking is a myth. Just as Abraham had faith and obeyed when God told him to leave his homeland and travel to a foreign land which was not known to him so that God's promise could be fulfilled [Genesis 12:1-5], so should you have such faith to trust and obey God in that which He is asking of you.

Each day you are presented with the *'Three C's of Life'* – *chances, choices and changes*. Every day, you have multiple chances to make different choices that will determine the changes in your life that will shape your future. What changes do you want to see in your life? What chances are being presented to you today? And what choices are you going to make to move forward? – Will you jump into the future that God has promised you and do what it takes to get there? Or will you retreat to your comfort zone because of the lies that the spirit of fear is whispering to you? Make choices that will lead you to freedom. Forget about risks, only have faith. Do not be afraid; jump towards success because God's plan is a good plan, one that will prosper you and not harm you [Jeremiah 29:11].

Day 10

YOU WILL MAKE IT!

"God will make this happen, for He who calls you is faithful"
– 1 Thessalonians 5:24 [NLT].

Sometimes your breakthroughs and successes are tightly wrapped up and packaged in hard work and placed on such high pedestals which may seem to be beyond your reach. That packaging is not attractive to you and the height of the pedestals makes them appear as though they are impossible to reach. Thoughts may start running through your mind about being "unrealistic" and to make it worse, you may not have the full support of those around you. Some friends or even family may tell you to stop day dreaming and come back down to earth. "Be realistic", they may say… don't let such negative vibes sway and distract you because until you unwrap the package, you won't know what is inside. When you finally get to unravel it, you come to understand why the opposition was so strong – it's because greatness was inside! Continue being "unrealistic" because with God that is realistic! Is there anything too hard for Him? With Christ, nothing is impossible! You have a Great God who cannot be predicted. His ways are not our ways [Isaiah 55:8] so, He is not limited by the logic and the things of the world. He is able to do exceedingly abundantly above anything you can ask or imagine [Ephesians 3:20].

Don't let anyone scare you into thinking that you're crazy for pursuing your dreams. In fact, be 'crazy' and let people talk; because, until you get called crazy for dreaming, then perhaps you're not dreaming big enough. God cannot be put in a box so keep dreaming bigger, not even the sky is your limit! Your 'craziness' is really showing the level of your faith; and faith is what pleases God. Rest assured that, no matter how big your vision is, God has an even bigger one and a plan for your life that will exceed your expectations; just allow Him to work through you. "No eye has seen, no ear has heard, and no mind has imagined what God has prepared for those who love Him." – 1 Corinthians 2:9 [NLT].

If God has said it and you align yourself with Him, then you will make it. He will surely bring all that He has placed in you to a successful and expected end. "So shall My word be that goes forth from My mouth; it shall not return to Me void, but it shall accomplish what I please, and it shall prosper in the thing for which I sent it" – Isaiah 55:11 [NKJV]. For His name sake (because you have used God's name), success is guaranteed. His name will not be used in vain. If it is truly of God, it will work regardless of the struggles you face, the hurdles you may have to jump and the length of time it may take; the result will always be successful.

Day 11

DON'T GIVE UP!

"Let us not grow weary or become discouraged in doing good, for at the proper time we will reap, if we do not give in"
– Galatians 6:9 [AMP].

You know those situations you go through that make you question, "what am I doing?" ... Bit by bit, you start losing your motivation and begin to ask yourself if it's even worth it. I've experienced it myself and seen others go through it too. Especially during dissertation season; I recall how many people just wanted to give up – they would cry out, saying: "I can't do this anymore" yet they were even on the verge of finishing the race. In the same way I encouraged them to stay focused and keep going, I want to do the same to you. Do not lose sight of the victory right that is coming your way; it's right ahead of you. Do not give up on your greater that is coming; that which you will receive when you reach the end of that tunnel. Stay focused on Jesus because it is in Him that you are victorious.

Losing sight of Jesus is what will cause you to start sinking because doubt will come in and start weighing you down. This is how the process of giving up begins. When Peter was walking on the water towards Jesus, everything was going well until he took his eyes off Jesus and on to the wind and waves instead which scared him and in turn, made him start sinking [Matthew 14:28-31]. Just like Peter, sometimes we experience situations in life that are a bit like the wind and the waves; they shake us and make us waver in our faith, causing us to stumble and dwell in unbelief. Why would Jesus invite Peter to walk on the water if He wouldn't keep him safe? Likewise, with your life – would God really put you somewhere or ask something of you if He knew that you couldn't handle it? Notice how Peter only started sinking when his attention was no longer on Jesus. You need to fix your eyes on Christ and press on towards the prize ahead of you; "I press on to reach the end of the race and receive the heavenly prize for which God, through Christ Jesus, is calling us" – Philippians 3:14 [NLT]. Be still and know that He is LORD over your life and over every situation you may face in your life.

The glory that God wants to give you is still worth fighting for. Fight a good fight and don't give up because the glory that you're about to receive is far greater than the pain you've endured. God does not start something without completing it; He is a finisher [Hebrews 12:2]. Be assured that the One Who has begun a good work in you will surely see you through until the very end [Philippians 1:6]. So, don't get tired and don't give up. This life is a race you must run and there is victory at the end of it.

"I have fought the good fight, I have finished the race, and I have remained faithful. And now the prize awaits me—the crown of righteousness, which the LORD, the Righteous Judge, will give me on the day of His return. And the prize is not just for me but for all who eagerly look forward to His appearing" – 2 Timothy 4:7-8 [NLT].

Day 12

YOU'RE IN TRAINING

"Enlarge the place of your tent, stretch your tent curtains wide, do not hold back; lengthen your cords, strengthen your stakes…"
– Isaiah 54:2 [NIV].

University is like a training ground that prepares you for the rest of your life because it is the season where you are away from home, you're responsible for making your own decisions, you meet all kinds of people and you grow in a vast number of ways. This is a key period in which you learn some lessons and establish some values that you will stand on as you progress in life. After university, you should have experience of how to budget and manage your money, work diligently, deal with different types of people and even the general house skills such as how to cook or use a washing machine! University is truly the transition stage where you start developing into the man or woman you want to be after university; it presents many opportunities to grow, so seize as many as you can so that you can be the best you, that you can be.

Before David killed Goliath, he had gone through his training when he killed the lion and the bear prior to that. "David said to Saul, "Your servant used to keep his father's sheep, and when a lion or a bear came and took a lamb… Your servant has killed both lion and bear; and this uncircumcised Philistine will be like one of them…" – 1 Samuel 17:34, 36 [NIV]. Even though David didn't know that one day he would slay a

The Young Christian at University

giant, he was already prepared because of what he had experienced in the field. In the same way, whatever you go through at university prepares you for what you will encounter further down the line and prepares you for your purpose. So, take note of the life lessons you are learning and that you will learn, desire to have more knowledge and wisdom so that you are prepared for the future.

Invest in your future, don't just live in the moment. Consider how your actions or your words will affect you in future. What are you doing right now to invest in your future? Are you actively seeking ways of improving yourself? How are you using your resources? There are so many things to consider but there's nothing to worry about because, if you involve God everything will work out; "seek His will in all you do, and He will show you which path to take" – Proverbs 3:6 [NLT].

As part of your training, look at the things God has intrusted you with. It may be a gift, it may be a talent or a passion for a specific thing etc. How are you using these things to affect change and glorify God? For example, if you have a large following on social media – such as Twitter or Instagram – are you misusing the platforms just to gain power, intimidate others? Leading people astray? Or are you utilising them wisely and productively – helping, inspiring, edifying others and bringing glory to God? The Bible tells us that, "…to whom much has been given, much will be required…" – Luke 12:48 [AMP]. Your faithfulness in small things is being tested now to see if you can be trusted to handle greater things later down the line. Don't abuse whatever God has entrusted to you now because a time will come when you will have to give an account for everything He gave you [Matthew 25:14-30]. Be fruitful.

DAY 13

STAND UP AND STAND OUT!

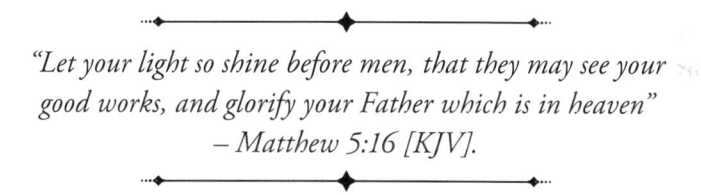

"Let your light so shine before men, that they may see your good works, and glorify your Father which is in heaven"
– Matthew 5:16 [KJV].

Jesus calls you the light of the world; therefore, you were created to stand out! You need to leave a mark on your university, don't just come and fade into the background.

God has placed so much in you that needs to be shared with the world. Your colleagues, lecturers, peers and friends should not be able to go without mentioning a time or the different ways in which you impacted their lives.

Whether it be your personality, your good deeds, what you believe in, your love for people or your heart for service; don't hide these great attributes. What do you stand for? If you don't stand for something, you will fall for anything. So be true to yourself and who God has created you to be; don't hide in the shadows or reduce yourself for the sake of not "outshining" others! You were created to shine so let your true self be seen so that God can get the glory due to Him! He's the One that put that light in you. Because Christ is in you, when you walk into a room, your presence should change the atmosphere - people should have the desire to find out what's so different about you and why you stand out from everybody else - in pursuit of that answer, they should find Christ! So, ask yourself this;

Are you shying away from displaying the true you that God created you to be? Or are you standing with boldness to defend your beliefs and living your fullest life?

Stop trying to fit in and don't worry about "what people will think". Don't be content with just attending lectures and going back home; there's so much ground for you to cover at university beyond the walls of your course! Don't just "go with the flow"; be extra, go over the top and get involved with different societies that bend the rules of the status quo. Never be afraid to ask questions about what you do not know or do not understand; it doesn't matter how you look to others - the truth is, someone else out there is sitting in the same boat as you, with the same burning questions but is too scared to speak up! Be vocal and make your university experience worthwhile. You don't want to look back and regret all the things you didn't do and wasted opportunities.

What will land you that dream job after university is not just your degree classification alone but the whole package wrapped up in your personality and experiences too. Maintain a positive attitude towards your learning and your daily life. Take risks and don't be content with mediocre! You are special and the world needs a sprinkle of your uniqueness.

Day 14

TRIALS AND TEMPTATIONS

"The temptations in your life are no different from what others experience. And God is faithful. He will not allow the temptation to be more than you can stand. When you are tempted, he will show you a way out so that you can endure"
– 1 Corinthians 10:13 [NLT]

Understand that temptations will surely come at some point, in your time of studies; not just then, but throughout your whole life. You will face temptations of many kinds. Even Jesus was tempted by the devil, we will inevitably be tempted as well. However, the fact that Jesus was able to overcome those temptations means that you can too. Rest assured that in your moment of temptation, God's grace is sufficient for you and He makes a way out for you so that you don't fall into the trap of the evil one.

There is nothing new under the sun, so just know that someone else has also been through what you're going through now – some people you know may even be going through the same thing at the same time. You are not alone in your struggle, God is indeed with you. Temptations can come in different forms; some of which you can control and others which may be beyond your control. As young people, sometimes we lead ourselves into temptation by engaging in activities we have no business engaging in, going to places we shouldn't be going to, watching things we shouldn't be watching or listening to things we shouldn't be listening to. Guard your heart [Proverbs 4:23]. Know your strength and don't deceive yourself in to thinking that you can handle what you know, deep down inside will be destructive and will end badly. Many slips are easily avoided. Stay true to yourself; stop trying to convince yourself that you're going to that girl or that guy's accommodation at 2am, by yourself to *"study"* or *"just to talk"*, don't say that you're *"going to the club to evangelise and to be a light"*, knowing full well that you're just going to do what everyone else is doing and partaking in the activities which may lead to other slip ups such as drinking or fornication. We may want, or claim to go to places with the intention to do good or save others, but we ourselves need saving. You can't be dancing with the devil and then not expect to fall into his traps. If you know that your flesh is weak, don't put yourself in compromising positions.

You should also be careful not lead your friends into temptation, for the Bible says, "there will always be temptations to sin, but what sorrow awaits the person who does the tempting!" – Luke 17:1 [NLT]. Let us learn to support one another for we are our brothers' keepers. May we sharpen one another [Proverbs 27:17] rather than leading each other astray and may God grant us the grace to overcome every trial and temptation so that we do not lose ourselves and hinder our faith.

DAY 15

DON'T WASTE TIME, EVERYDAY COUNTS

"Don't let the excitement of youth cause you to forget your Creator. Honour him in your youth before you grow old and say, "Life is not pleasant anymore"
– Ecclesiastes 12:1 [NLT].

Time is so precious. The thing is, once time is gone… its gone, there's no going back or rewinding time. This scripture talks about remembering God in the days of your youth and there must be a very good reason as to why it admonishes us in such a way. I've seen and heard several people in university say; *"let me have my fun and enjoy my time now, then I will give myself fully to God later and do His work then"*. However, the fact remains that, "later" is not promised. How do you know how long you will live? You must to be ready to meet your Maker at all times because anything can happen at any time or Jesus could return at any moment. Your life is far too valuable to spend it on the world – don't waste your time on things carnal things that will not get you to heaven; "don't waste your time on useless work, mere busywork, the barren pursuits of darkness. Expose these things for the sham they are. It's a scandal when people waste their lives on things they must do in the darkness where no one will see" – Ephesians 5:11-12 [MSG]. Focus on your relationship with Christ, your spiritual growth, growth in other areas of your life and on whatever He's calling you to do for His Kingdom.

There's a popular saying that states, *"those who fail to plan also plan to fail"*. Take advantage of every given day and work diligently to fulfil the destiny which God has set out for you. Don't waste valuable time procrastinating and doing other things that don't edify when you can use it wisely chasing your dreams, pursuing your purpose and advancing the Kingdom. A lot of people like to "live in the moment", spending time and doing things that only give their flesh temporary pleasure for a moment instead of working on those things that will give rise to eternal joy. Spend your youthful years building towards the destiny God has set out for you; start walking in alignment with Him as early as possible so that you can live the best, fruitful life possible. Now is the time that you're still strong and full of energy; as you age energy becomes sparse and the demands of life increase – so, it will get harder to do certain things that you can do now, when you're older. Work hard now so that you can relax and enjoy the fruits of your labour later; both on earth and in heaven.

"I said, 'Plant the good seeds of righteousness, and you will harvest a crop of love. Plow up the hard ground of your hearts, for now is the time to seek the LORD, that He may come and shower righteousness upon you.' "But you have cultivated wickedness and harvested a thriving crop of sins. You have eaten the fruit of lies…" [NLT] "…you have eaten the fruit of deception. Because you have depended on your own strength and on your many warriors…" [NIV] – Hosea 10:12-13.

Day 16

STARTING OVER AGAIN

"Then Jesus said, "Come to Me, all of you who are weary and carry heavy burdens, and I will give you rest. Take My yoke upon you. Let Me teach you, because I am humble and gentle at heart, and you will find rest for your souls. For My yoke is easy to bear, and the burden I give you is light"
– Matthew 11:28-30 [NLT].

When you have reached breaking point – the point where it feels like all hope is gone and there is no way out of your mess – that is when it's time to hit the reset button and start all over again. Perhaps you got to this point because you started spending less and less time with God as time went by? Well, its time you come back to The Source of Life and strength. No matter how deep your situation has become, God is able to revive you from even from the point of death and restore you back to vibrant life. He wants you to come to Him and rest in Him. Sometimes we feel like we cannot go back to God because of our sins or what we've done; we feel unworthy of His love. Note that these are lies and tactics of the enemy adopted only to stop you from plucking up the courage to go back to God and start again. "And I am convinced that nothing can ever separate us from God's love. Neither death nor life, neither angels nor demons, neither our fears for today nor our worries about tomorrow—not even the powers of hell can separate us from God's love. No power in the sky above or in the earth below—indeed, nothing in all creation will ever be able to separate us from the love of God that is revealed in Christ Jesus our LORD" – Romans 8:38-39 [NLT].

The truth is, sometimes God has to break you in order to make you and build you up again. It is the breaking that gives you the strength, wisdom and courage to press forward for the making. When He breaks you, it's not to hurt you but to make you stronger than ever before. He needs your undivided attention, that is why He will allow certain things to happen; that way, you realise in your own strength you can't help yourself – you also realise that you have no one to turn to but Him. So, when you feel like life has gotten tough and the stress of university has overtaken you, press reboot and go back to your Father in heaven. All the Father wants is for you to understand that you need Him and that you need to seek Him for strength. When you're broken, He will heal, purify and restore you.

DAY 17

STOP AND RECHARGE

"Truly my soul finds rest in God; my salvation comes from Him. Truly He is my rock and my salvation; He is my fortress, I will never be shaken"
– Psalm 62:1-2 [NIV].

As children of God who are called to serve and sharpen one another as iron does, it is a fact that whatever you have inside of you, is what you eventually give out and pour into others whether it be through teaching, giving advice, praying with others, visiting the sick, helping the poor and needy or checking up on people etc. that is why it so important that you take some time out to recharge in God's presence. You can't pour from an empty cup! You do not want to get weary and burned out then start to resent the work of God. Don't turn it into a burden just because you are neglecting the relationship aspect. Always take time to bask in God's presence each day. If you are constantly giving out but fail to top up, you will eventually have nothing to give anymore.

What comes out of you is what defiles you [Matthew 5:11] – so, what comes out of your mouth is based on what is inside of you; "a good person produces good things from the treasury of a good heart, and an evil person produces evil things from the treasury of an evil heart. What you say flows from what is in your heart" – Luke 6:45 [NLT]. What is inside of you is based on what you feed your soul and your spirit. So, what is stored in your heart? Wat is it you're feeding your spirit? Especially if you're not taking out the time to recharge...

Just as you feed your body when you are hungry, you ought to feed your spirit with the things of God. Do not starve the Spirit; eat the Word. As you feed the Spirit, you increase the capacity for God to take over and use your life. There should be more of God and less of you, particularly if you want to operate in the gifts of the Spirit. You must be in tune with the Holy Spirit to speak the mind of God. The flesh is self-seeking and leads to sin but the Spirit speaks all truth and leads you in the way to eternal life. Let God increase as you decrease for the manifestation of His Spirit in your life.

Another thing to remember is that before anything else, you are a child of God – so don't neglect your relationship with Him. It's great to spread the gospel and share Christ with everyone so that they can go to heaven. But don't neglect your own walk with God that you miss heaven yourself. "I discipline my body like an athlete, training it to do what it should. Otherwise, I fear that after preaching to others I myself might be disqualified" – 1 Corinthians 9:27 [NLT]. Make sure you're taking the time to stop and recharge in His presence to ensure that you're on the right track too – not just to get a message for the masses – but to also be transformed yourself.

Day 18

HELPING OTHERS

"Each of you should use whatever gift you have received to serve others, as faithful stewards of God's grace in its various forms"
– 1 Peter 4:10 [NIV].

The gifts that God has given you are not just for your own benefit but also for the benefit of other people. But most importantly, for the glory of God. Depending on what your gifting is, there are so many ways in which you could serve others. For example, if you are very confident at public speaking, you can use that gift to help develop people who lack confidence, or to inspire, motivate and encourage others. Other gifts may be useful for the raising up of Kingdom leaders, helping the homeless, spreading hope and joy and just so many other things; the possibilities are endless. Just as someone could benefit from your gifts, you could also benefit from someone else's gifts.

As believers, our prime purpose is to bring the world to the saving knowledge of Christ so that they may receive salvation. Depending on what God has placed in each of us as individuals, we all have different ways in which to accomplish this mission. Your purpose is found in your mission of bringing souls to Jesus Christ. Now this mission is fulfilled by utilising the different gifts that God has placed in you. Helping others is an integral part of achieving your purpose. If all your dreams, gifts and ideas do not help or impact people for the better or glorify God, know that they may be coming from a place of selfish ambition. Likewise, if what you are doing only benefits the world and promotes fleshly things such as sexual immorality, drunkenness, deceit, gossip, slander, violence, love of money and other carnal behaviours then it's all done in vain and you are misusing the gifts that God has given you. Use your gifts so that souls can be saved and that God's glory can be made manifest in the earth.

"Go therefore and make disciples of all the nations [help the people to learn of Me, believe in Me, and obey My words], baptizing them in the name of the Father and of the Son and of the Holy Spirit" –Matthew 28:19 [AMP]. Look around you, how are you helping and impacting the lives of those around you?

Day 19

HUNGER FOR IT

"And from the days of John the Baptist until now the kingdom of heaven suffers violence, and the violent take it by force"
– Matthew 11:12 [NKJV].

As God begins to reveal your purpose as you go on an identity search, you find that He places big dreams on your heart. Those God-dreams and ideas are the big, crazy ones that seem almost impossible. They must be big so that His glory can be shown in a mighty way – but they are not impossible, maybe on your own – yes – but not with Christ. He promises to equip you for whatever He has called you to do; "may he equip you with all you need for doing His will. May He produce in you, through the power of Jesus Christ, every good thing that is pleasing to Him" – Hebrews 13:21 [NLT]. So, nothing is really stopping you from walking in purpose; you are equipped, the Holy Spirit is backing you and the devil has already been defeated – he will still try his luck at knocking you off course but God has given you the necessary armour and weapons to deal with him. So really and truly, the only thing that can stand between you and fulfilling your destiny is yourself.

How hungry are you to achieve your dreams?

Yes, you may speak about it daily – and yes, you may surely have a tonne of world changing ideas – but how far are you willing to go to accomplish the tasks God has given you? How much work and effort are you willing to put in? What are the sacrifices you are willing to make to reach your goals? Are you prepared to lose sleep over it? Are you willing to give up the pleasure of your youth to work towards the goals for the future? What if people don't believe in your dreams – do you leave it and get disheartened or do you fight for what you know God has entrusted to you? Can anything stand between you and your dreams? If you had to lose friends and family to achieve what God has called you to, would you still do it? – these are just a few possible questions that can help gauge just how hungry you truly are to see God's purpose for your life to manifest. Answer them truthfully so that you can get on the right track towards destiny.

The main scripture mentions that the Kingdom of God suffers violence – why do you think that opposition is so prevalent when it comes to fulfilling purpose? The enemy knows that your God-dream is linked to the salvation of many souls who will be snatched out of the kingdom of darkness and brought into God's Kingdom of Light; ultimately giving God the glory – which is why you need to approach your dreams with a violent zeal and passion. Let nothing get in the way of your destiny! It is much bigger than you. Take. It. By. Force.

Aside from taking it by force physically by taking action, you also need to take it by force spiritually because spiritual warfare is real. Are you diligently praying about the things God has revealed you and seeking His face for more guidance, direction and strategies or is your prayer life idle? Are you reading the Word for deeper revelation and understanding or is your Bible closed? Are you fasting to subdue your flesh and strengthen your spirit so that you are strongly in tune with God, or are you indulging your flesh and starving your spirit? Hungering for and seeking after things of the Spirit puts you in a better position to receive and overflow of God's divine Power to help you live out His plan for your life.

Day 20

DO NOT SETTLE FOR MEDIOCRE

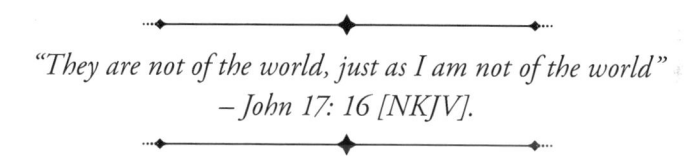

"They are not of the world, just as I am not of the world"
– John 17: 16 [NKJV].

When everyone is smoking weed, getting drunk at parties and having sex regularly – just because everyone else is doing it; remember, you don't have to get involved with such because though you are in the world, you're not of it. Understand what you stand for, Who you represent and Whose name you carry. Do not get comfortable doing what everyone else is doing at university. "Don't copy the behaviour and customs of this world, but let God transform you into a new person by changing the way you think. Then you will learn to know God's will for you, which is good and pleasing and perfect" – Romans 12:2 [NLT].

You can't be in two minds because God has an assignment for you to accomplish in your university. He has an assignment for you to accomplish in the lives of your friends, your colleagues and even your lecturers. So, unless you are sober, you will never know what God is doing in each season He brings you into or understand His will for your life at a given time. If you say you are His, then be fully His – you can't be half in and half out, half with God and half with the devil; it doesn't work that way. You can't serve two masters [Matthew 6:24]. "I know all the things you do, that you are neither hot nor cold. I wish that you were one or the other! But since you are like lukewarm water, neither hot nor cold, I will spit you out of my mouth!" – Revelation 3:15-16 [NLT].

God is not a mediocre God; therefore, you can't live a mediocre life – that's not what you have been called to. You have been called to live an extraordinary life, one in which you walk in power; Jesus said, "…you will receive power when the Holy Spirit comes upon you. And you will be My witnesses, telling people about Me everywhere…" – Acts 1:8 [NLT]. Stay away from the meaningless, time wasting activities that everyone else is indulging in and don't follow the crowd. Get in the habit of seeking the LORD's face daily so that you know what His will is; then you will be able to take the necessary steps for partnering with Him towards greatness and making His name known. Don't settle for safe and don't settle for average; aim to be on top form in every area of your life.

"Do your best to present yourself to God as one approved, a worker who has no need to be ashamed, rightly handling the word of truth" – 2 Timothy 2:15 [ESV].

Day 21

DO IT TODAY!

"So, prepare your minds for action, be completely sober [in spirit—steadfast, self-disciplined, spiritually and morally alert] ..."
– 1 Peter 1:13 [AMP].

So many people have world changing ideas that they are sitting on because they are waiting for the *'perfect'* opportunity to take action. Don't let that be you… When *is* the *right time* or the *perfect opportunity*? If you are always waiting for *'that time'*, your ideas will continue gathering dust on the shelf. The late Dr Myles Monroe said that the graveyard is the richest place on earth because, not only are dead people buried there, but also all the dreams, visions, books, ideas, businesses, cures to diseases, songs and plans etc., that they had within them but were never brought into fruition – so many purposes never realised. World changing ideas that could have saved lives and so much more, gone forever. What ideas have you been sitting on? You never know, it may change the face of the world as we know it – whether it be in the areas of education, politics, business, entertainment or whatever sector God has given you a burden for.

You never know how many times an opportunity is going to present itself to you; some opportunities are once in a lifetime. So, do everything you can to grab them with both hands, especially now whilst you're young and whilst you have the time and energy. Do you have any fresh innovative business ideas in mind? What are you doing with the gifts God has given you? The Parable of the Talents [Matthew 25:14-30] is an illustration of what will happen on Judgement Day. You will have to give God an account for the life you lived on earth; He will want to know what you did with the love, gifts, talents, resources and everything else that He put in you for carrying out His work on earth of spreading the Gospel and making His name known to redirect the lost back into His Kingdom. Do you know what you will answer Him? You don't want to be the wicked and lazy servant who is cast away to perish, but rather a good and faithful servant who will share in His joy and enter glory ... So, what are you waiting for? If you haven't yet started doing something about it already, start now whilst you're at university or wherever you are at right now; it's the perfect time to commence.

The fact that you're reading means that you have the privilege of being alive; there is still purpose in you! Take advantage of each opportunity that comes your way and seize each God given day because you don't know what tomorrow may bring. "We must quickly carry out the tasks assigned us by the one who sent us. The night is coming, and then no one can work" – John 9:4 [NLT].

Ask yourself this, what is actually stopping you from starting the work that God wants you to do? It's very easy to make excuses as you why you *"can't"* do something but the Bible says that you *can* do ALL things through Christ who strengthens you [Philippians 4:13]. For every excuse, there is a solution – but you must be willing to moved forward and get started. Cut out the procrastination. "So be careful how you live. Don't live like fools, but like those who are wise. Make the most of every opportunity in these evil days. Don't act thoughtlessly, but understand what the LORD wants you to do" – Ephesians 5:15-17 [NLT]. It is foolish and unwise to procrastinate, it is also a sin; "remember, it is sin to know what you ought to do and then not do it" – James 4:17 [NLT]. Cast down every though and lie that says you *"can't"* in the name of Jesus; God will not tell you to do something without equipping you or providing the resources [Hebrews 13:21]. It's now just about being disciplined enough to carry out the task and steps towards the goal daily. Rome wasn't built in a day, so don't expect to have reached your destination overnight; taking steps each day will ensure that you get there – whereas staying stagnant and doing nothing delays your destiny. Start NOW! Start today!

Printed in Great Britain
by Amazon